Marketing Through Minefields

HBR Case Studies Series

Every day, managers face challenges that put them to the test. When it comes to the thorniest dilemmas, there's never just one right answer. Get the guidance you need from our new HBR Case Studies series. Straight from the pages of the *Harvard Business Review*, each book breaks down your most familiar—and formidable—business problems: you'll get six engaging scenarios, each with several detailed solutions by today's leading experts. Read the cases, gain more perspective, and hone your instincts—so you can finalize your plan and move forward successfully.

Other books in the series

HBR CASE STUDIES

Marketing Through Minefields

Harvard Business Press

Boston, Massachusetts

Copyright 2008 Harvard Business School Publishing Corporation
All rights reserved
Printed in the United States of America
12 11 10 09 08   5 4 3 2 1

ISBN: 978-1-4221-9992-3

Cataloging-in-Publication Data is available for this title.

The paper used in this publication meets the requirements of the American
National Standard for Permanence of Paper for Publications and Documents
in Libraries and Archives Z39.48-1992.

CONTENTS

Marketing Through Minefields

Introduction

In that great musical comedy *How to Succeed in Business Without Really Trying*, we see an ambitious young businessman ascending quickly through the corporate ranks by following the Machiavellian advice of a how-to manual. All goes well through the end of the first act, when he engineers the dismissal of the vice president of advertising and inherits the man's job. But then, ready to take another step toward the corner office, he turns the page of his book. The next chapter, he finds, is entitled: "What To Do If You Make a Mistake and Find Yourself Vice President of Advertising."

Managing the marketing function, the play makes clear, can only mean peril. That was a well-enough-known truth to get a big laugh on Broadway in 1961—

and it's probably even truer today. If anything, the stakes are higher, the options more numerous, and the repercussions of unwise decisions more daunting than ever.

What are the minefields a marketer wanders into? Famously, they consist of four big pieces of territory. In Jerome McCarthy's classic formulation, these are the 4 P's: product (including all the features, like service and packaging, attached to what you sell); place (referring to distribution channels); promotion (all forms of communication with customers); and price (including discounts, pricing flexibility, and so forth). Whether you accept his terminology or prefer Phillip Kotler's more customer-centric version—he recast them all to begin with C's—it's a lot of ground to cover. A misstep in any one of these areas can wipe out the profits generated by the other three. And despite the fact that marketing is steadily becoming less of a pure "art" and more of a science, the judgment calls managers must make are still highly subjective.

That's why, at *Harvard Business Review*, we devote so many of our case studies to marketing topics. It's not just that they make for good reading; more important, marketing offers true dilemmas—situations in which smart people can disagree dramatically on how to proceed, and no path forward is without risk.

How to Learn from a Case Study Without Really Trying

HBR's Case Study is the longest-running department in the magazine's 80-plus year history, and with good reason. Appearing at the front of each issue, the case presents an engaging piece of fiction—a story of a manager facing a problem—and then asks distinguished commentators to weigh in with insights and advice.

It's a highly educational format, because it compels readers to think through the problem and formulate a response for themselves. As editors, we select case topics and commentators specifically to ensure some difference of opinion; we studiously avoid providing the "right answer" at the end. In fact, many readers prefer to pause after reading the story, decide how they think the dilemma should be resolved, and then proceed to discover which piece of expert advice aligns with their thinking. (Sometimes none does, and that can be even more satisfying.)

In addition to providing a training tool for managers, HBR case studies often break new ground, especially when previous experience and existing knowledge are sparse. A case study can look at the problem from multiple angles, explore its nuances, and begin to pinpoint the aspects of the phenomenon that could be fruitfully researched. In the expert commentaries that follow each case study, we may see the beginnings of a framework for addressing an emerging area of concern. That, in any case, has been the hope behind several of the marketing-related cases we've published recently.

Marketing Mix-Ups

For this collection, we have chosen case studies that raise thorny issues in each of the 4 P's of marketing.

Under the heading of product, we explore the question of whether to match an enhancement made by a major competitor—even though customers say they don't need it ("The Quality Improvement Customers Didn't Want"). In the category of place, we look at the channel opportunities presented to a company with a hot property to license ("License to Overkill"). Our cases on promotion explore issues of PR crisis management ("When No News Is Good News"), global branding ("The Global Brand Face-Off"), and sports event sponsorship ("Keeping to the Fairway"). Finally, we include a dilemma in pricing, as a company struggles with whether to offer a differentiated level of service—at a higher price point—to its most affluent customers ("Are Some Customers More Equal Than Others?"). So where should you start? If you're a student of marketing in general, you'd do well to read them all, but the brief synopses that follow help you decide which one to read first.

When No News Is Good News

This case by Bronwyn Fryer depicts every consumer product company's nightmare: an injured child—as a result of an incident involving the company's product—a media frenzy, and a public relations disaster spiraling out of control. In the case of baby stroller manufacturer BestBaby Corporation, it scarcely helps that the cause was probably user error and not actual product failure. The parents of three-month-old Avery Nelkin are famous and wealthy, and as the child lies in an intensive care unit, reporters are playing the story for all it's worth. To make matters much worse, an employee long in the habit of expressing inflammatory, and sometimes unfounded, quality warnings reminds management of a memo she wrote months ago on the possibility of brake failure. Greg James, CEO of BestBaby, pulls his executive team together immediately to figure out what to say to the world that afternoon—and how to redeem his company's reputation in the days to come.

The first commentator on the case, John Hall, has experience with PR crisis management. As former chairman of Ashland Incorporated, he presided over his company's response when one of its storage tanks collapsed in 1988, spilling diesel fuel into the Monongahela and Ohio Rivers. He urges Greg to openly state all the facts he has—rather than leave them for a reporter to discover later. USC professor Ian Mitroff, author of *Managing Crises Before They Happen*, wants Greg to ask himself: What illness existed within our corporation structure that allowed this to happen? He believes there were warning signs leading up to the crisis—if only a proactive crisis-management team had been in place to see them. Robin Cohn, author of *The PR Crisis Bible*, notes that the company is already late in getting out a media statement. A voluntary recall is the best first move, she says. And that's the strategy that would satisfy the fourth commentator, too. Alan Schoem directs the U.S. Consumer Product Safety Commission's compliance office, and he outlines details of what such a recall would entail.

Are Some Customers More Equal Than Others?

There's been a tremendous movement in the past several years toward discriminatory, or tiered, pricing—that is, where certain classes of customers pay higher rates for a product or service, usually in return for some extra amenities that are of particular value to them. (Famously, on airlines, business travelers and pleasure travelers are charged vastly different sums for their seats.) This case, by Paul Nunes and Brian Johnson, was designed to explore the issues raised by such pricing. They chose to set it in a theme-park business, where the possibility being discussed is a "preferred guest card" that would, for a substantial fee, allow a customer to jump the queues on rides and get fast seating in the parks' restaurants. Paradise Parks' CFO is keen on the idea as a way of capturing more wealth from affluent, time-pressed customers, without pricing the park out of reach for its lower-income mainstays. But Jill Hoover, CEO of the company, finds the idea vaguely repugnant, especially in light of the democratic ideals on which her father founded the company.

John Harrington, former CEO of the Boston Red Sox, tells Jill she'll have to get over that attitude, just as he did. To make the money required to cover today's outrageous player salaries, he says, "we increasingly focused on the customers who were willing to pay more." And it was the only way to keep the lowest-priced bleacher seats as cheap as possible at the same time. The second commentator, Edward Goldman, makes the point that "America is still a place where people can make money and spend it the way they want." His business, MDVIP, is a medical practice that charges high prices, and can therefore keep doctors' caseloads low. Despite charges that it undermines the health care system's ability to serve the poor adequately, he believes that people who value more attentive care should have the option to buy it. Alexander Labak, CMO at Deutsche Bank, agrees that it simply makes good business sense to segment customers and offer different levels of service at the upper end of the market. In his business it's called Private Banking. Following a "one size fits all" strategy is, in most cases, a recipe for disaster. But Bob Crandall, legendary former chairman of American Airlines, notes that any service differentiation will have to be done with subtlety. "The business will surely suffer," he says, "if the average customer goes to the park and finds he can't get on the best rides because the place is full of conventioneers who are entitled to jump the line."

License to Overkill

This second case by Paul Nunes defines a rather narrow problem—property licensing—but one that is increasingly a part of the marketer's existence. The U.S. licensing market is already a $70 billion industry. The International Licensing Show, which had fewer than 150 attendees when it began in the mid-1980s, now attracts more than 10,000 visitors and 500 exhibitors. Here the manager with a decision to make is Sheldon Bloomfield, who works for the property management agency. He's promoting "Baby Ruby"—a sort of Raggedy Ann for the twenty-first century—which started as a series of books but is now winning over American television audiences. Sheldon has a movie deal in the works, is deep in negotiations with a fast-food chain to do a tie-in toy line for its kids' meals, and is courting numerous other opportunities to put Ruby's likeness on merchandise. He faces a difficult decision, though, when the offers come in lower than he'd like. Should he strike while the property is hot and take everything he can get? Or does Ruby have what it takes to be an "evergreen" property—in which case he should be careful to avoid overexposure in these early days?

The first commentator, cultural studies scholar Grant McCracken, notes that there is nothing quite as unappealing as last week's fast-food promotion. He says that Sheldon "needs to let his evergreens grow for a while, before he starts trimming them with junk." Jack Soden, CEO of Elvis Presley Enterprises, manages a property that is certainly not an overnight fad. His advice? Get on a plane, meet again with Baby Ruby's author, and secure the rights to the rest of the world (not just the North American rights Sheldon already has). Then play hardball with the studio over the terms of the deal—and at the same time get more involved in promoting the book series. Timothy Rothwell, an executive in Universal Studios Consumer Products Group, says the dilemma set up by the case is wrong: You don't have to choose between building an ever-green brand and signing lots of deals now. In fact, those deals are needed to push Baby Ruby to the level where she'll have staying power. Finally, we include the voice of an author who has a marketable property: Bill Griffith, creator of the comic strip *Zippy the Pinhead*. "For me," he writes, "the most disturbing part of this case was how easily the artist . . . signed away all of her licensing rights." He makes an observation that could apply equally to Sheldon: "if you give everything away at the beginning, it's all over."

The Global Brand Face-Off

Anand Raman's case study combines two hot topics in marketing: product placement and global branding. The global marketing officer of Espoir Cosmetics wants to see her company's products featured promi-nently in a film that's bound to be a blockbuster. But the deal is so pricey, it will only make sense economi-cally if she can get Espoir's marketing heads worldwide to go along with the promotion. To suit the realities of different markets, the company has always allowed its marketing mix to be highly customized by local management; this new venture would be a way to launch a truly global brand-building strategy. As the case closes, the GMO, Natasha Singh, has lined up support for her plan from some major regions—but the head of the company's Eastern European operations is dead against it. And her CEO is wondering whether a global brand even makes sense.

Peter Thompson, president and CEO of PepsiCo Beverages International, says Singh has the right idea, but should have started earlier with her efforts to get the local managers to align with a global initiative. He offers four pieces of advice, including a suggestion that she create a "menu" allowing some local choices. Stanford professor Jennifer Aaker points out the difference between strategy and execution in global brand-building. She cites Intel's practice of setting global goals at headquarters, but leaving control over execution of campaigns to local managers. Two executives from Unilever, Harish Manwani and Simon Clift, mirror the roles portrayed in this case; one is in charge of Latin American marketing while the other works at headquarters. They admit it's hard to strike the "right balance between being mindlessly global and hopelessly local," and say the most important thing to get right is the structure of the marketing organization. Temple University's Mike Kotabe, who literally wrote the book on *Global Marketing Management*, makes an interesting point about globalization: that, for consumers, it means freedom from conformity, as they can chose products from all over the world. A one-size-fits-all global strategy might not be effective.

The Quality Improvement Customers Didn't Want

In Dawn Iacobucci's case, the management of HMO Quality Care is struggling with the question of whether to introduce a technology-enabled service enhancement. The biggest players in the industry are doing it, and the management consultant the company hired to investigate the possibility is gung-ho, despite the substantial cost. The only problem is that Quality Care's marketing staff has already asked customers if they would value this innovation—essentially, automated reception and registration—and they've said no. When it comes to their medical care, they prefer the human touch. Allan Moulter, CEO of Quality Care, recognizes that there may be benefits that customers just aren't anticipating; by taking care of routine busywork, the new technology could free staff up for other interactions with patients. One thing is certain: Quality Care leads the industry in customer retention, and Moulter doesn't want to make a decision that will screw that up.

Thomas Jones of Elm Square Technologies, which markets customer-service software, says it's "a no brainer": Quality Care should develop and install the new reception system. When customers are asked for feedback on a proposed change, he cautions, managers should not put too much stock in their responses. But an opposing view comes from Arizona State University associate professor Mary Jo Bitner, coauthor of *Services Marketing*. She isn't sure that the new system would really serve customers well. The CEO, she says, "needs to think about how an automated reception encounter would affect his customers, who may be arriving for their appointments sick, unsure of themselves, and emotionally vulnerable." Eric Hanselman from Bay Networks warns Quality Care not to be overly dazzled by a system that's working well for a competitor. It needs to examine its own goals and plan the system that is right for it. Christopher Swan of British Airways concurs. He suspects that Quality Care's competitors might have had reasons for installing the systems other than enhancing customer care. Finally, Teresa Swartz, a marketing professor at CalTech, is most vehement that the voice of the customer needs to be respected. Why not, she suggests, forge a win-win solution? Quality Care should institute an advanced system for its frontline employees to use with patients.

Keeping to the Fairway

The last case in the collection, by Tom Waite, focuses on what is perhaps the fastest-growing practice in marketing today: sports and other event sponsorship. In the months leading up to the playing of the 2003 Masters

Tournament (the most prestigious competition in American golf), controversy erupted over the fact that the club where it would be played, Augusta National, did not have any women as members. This case examines a similar situation and raises the question of how the top sponsors of the event—mega corporations with important clients to entertain and also mass markets to woo—should react to the criticism. Is this a question of ethics? Or simply a question of marketing communications? Will the whole controversy blow over in a few months, as the public's attention moves to other things? And in that case, does it make sense to pull the plug on a multi-year sponsorship that has yielded many benefits?

Sergio Zyman, former chief marketing officer of Coca-Cola and now a marketing consultant, sympathizes with Pace Sterling, the company at the center of this case. But he doesn't see that it has many options. "I can tell you," he says, "in the real world, if the head of the nation's most powerful women's organization puts public pressure on you to walk away from a sponsorship, you walk." His counterpart at Accenture, Jim Murphy, says it's essential that the company get a better sense of how its clients feel about the controversy. Even in the tight time frame described by the case, the company's executives could use the Internet to conduct a customer survey. Kim Skildum-Reid, coauthor of *The Sponsor's Toolkit*, warns Pace Sterling that "To a much greater extent than other marketing media, sponsorships communicate what the brand values. . . ." A company that associates with a sexist organization is saying something about itself. Professor Paul Argenti of Dartmouth strongly agrees—to the point that he suggests firing the CMO who wants to keep the sponsorship in force. "She needs to remember," he says, "that her job isn't to teach a civics lesson on the right of free assembly but instead to enhance her company's reputation."

Honing Good Judgment

Will reading these cases make you a better marketer? I think so—provided you put yourself in the protagonists' shoes, engage the issues, and think critically about the best path forward. That, after all, is the basis of the case method, and fundamental to most professional learning.

In a commentary on a 2003 case study, Steve Kaufman, the retired chairman of Arrow Electronics, passed along some advice his father gave him as a young man. "Good judgment comes from experience," he said. "But unfortunately, experience comes from bad judgment." Perhaps that's overstating things a bit. With tools like the *Harvard Business Review* Case Study, managers can develop their judgment without the expense of career-limiting gaffes. Think of it as a management simulator—the equivalent of the fake Boeings and Airbuses that airline pilots use to become proficient.

Indeed, armed with the advice of this slim volume, you might even be able to survive a career in marketing. It's been done before. Think of J. Pierpont Finch, the hero of *How to Succeed in Business Without Really Trying*. Finch dealt handily with his boss's desire to see his talent-free girlfriend in the company's ads—a marketing dilemma of the first order. And he ended up with the chairmanship of the company, the girl of his dreams, and new aspirations—for the U.S. presidency. It's a wonderful thing, the power of a good management book. Now get reading.

When No News

Is Good News

Executive Summary

For as long as can be remembered, BestBaby Corporation, a manufacturer of baby equipment and furniture, has enjoyed a solid reputation with retailers, a good track record with consumers, and a supportive relationship with stockholders. But then the child of a celebrity is injured when her stroller tips over because its brakes failed. The media go wild, and CEO Greg James finds himself in uncharted territory.

The morning after the accident, Greg calls an emergency meeting of his executive staff. As he searches his memory to prepare for it, he thinks about Arzep Enterprises, BestBaby's main provider of parts and materials. He remembers his COO, Keith

Sigismund, telling him that Arzep had switched suppliers at some point in order to cut its own costs. Nevertheless, Keith had assured Greg that the new material, although not quite as sturdy, hadn't affected the quality of Arzep's components.

By the time the meeting is set to begin, several employees have threatened to quit, and stories are surfacing in the press and on the Web about other consumers who have had problems with their strollers. Then in the meeting, Keith drops a bombshell: he reads from a year-old memo sent to him by an employee in manufacturing stating that the new brake fittings delivered by Arzep don't grab the front brakes as well as the ones previously supplied. The same employee, and others, had complained in the past that Keith hadn't adequately attended to concerns they brought up to him.

In this fictional case study, four commentators offer advice to Greg on how BestBaby should respond to the victim's family, the media, the public, and the company's own employees during this PR crisis.

Greg James punched the button on the Lexus's stereo, scanning the stations for the morning news story he didn't want to hear. Sure enough, 101.7 was in mid-broadcast, playing that cratchy, dramatic 911 recording. "Help! The baby!" a young woman shrieked. "She's—oh, she's hurt her head! She's bleeding all over! Oh, my God—it's not my fault!"

A fresh wave of nausea hit Greg as he forced himself to listen for an update on the situation. "As we reported yesterday evening, the injured child is Avery Nelkin, the three-month-old daughter of Academy Award winners Nick Nelkin and Celia Winston. She remains in critical condition, and doctors are uncertain whether she will recover from injuries sustained when her stroller rolled down the driveway of the Nelkins' Laurel Canyon home."

The broadcast continued as Greg turned into the BestBaby parking lot. "Caught by reporters this morning at the hospital, Mr. Nelkin continued to lay blame for the incident on the manufacturer of the stroller— BestBaby Corporation of Des Moines, Iowa—and implied he will initiate legal action against it. So far, the company has not commented. We will continue to update you throughout the day."

Greg winced and clicked off the radio. It was all like a bad dream. Throughout the previous evening, that horrible 911 recording—and Nelkin's threatened lawsuit—had been inescapable headline news. Greg sighed wearily as he eased into the reserved parking spot. "It's obvious that I'll make some kind of announcement today," he said to himself. "But what should I say?"

Greg found Jane Benson, the company's public relations manager, waiting for him in the lobby. She wondered whether he'd heard about the recall demands. She grabbed his elbow. "Greg, we've got a *huge* problem here," she said in a low, tense voice. "My phone's been ringing off the hook. CNN and ABC News have both left messages on my voice mail. Their crews are on the way. They've asked for a statement from you. I haven't returned any calls yet." She paused briefly, gauging Greg's deepening frown. "And I—I've been checking the Web. Three sites are running headlines calling us 'WorstBaby.' This morning, Consumerwatch posted something on its Web page, asking users whether they think we should recall the stroller. It's already logged more than a hundred responses saying we should. People are swapping stories about accidents with our strollers. We simply have to come up with a response, and pronto."

"Call an all-hands emergency meeting," Greg responded. "I want all executive staff in the boardroom in an hour. We'll give everyone a full briefing. Don't worry," he said compassionately, scanning Jane's worried expression. "We'll get this under control."

What Went Wrong?

"Everything's happening so fast," Greg thought as the elevator doors closed. "The Nelkin accident occurred yesterday evening. Now all these angry people are coming out of the woodwork with broken-stroller stories. Funny they didn't say anything before." He pursed his lips. "I haven't even had time to figure out what's happened, let alone consider a recall. And now," he thought bitterly, "it looks like the Consumer Product Safety Commission may make that decision for me."

Greg searched his memory. In the ten years he'd spent running BestBaby, he had never confronted a bona fide PR crisis. Indeed, as far as public relations was concerned, the company had always had a good track record. In 1975, the company's cofounder and former CEO, Simon Levison, had asked him to join BestBaby as head of sales, handpicking Greg from a raft of brilliant candidates. After serving as vice president of sales and marketing and later as COO, Greg found himself in the CEO spot when Levison kicked himself upstairs to the chairmanship.

After 20 years at BestBaby, Greg had been overjoyed to take on the position. He loved children; he and his wife had three grandchildren. He felt like he'd trained his whole life to run a company that catered to little ones. Greg knew the 1,200-employee company intimately after having spent so many years running sales and operations. He felt that BestBaby was really his baby: he took personal pride in the company's excellent reputation as a manufacturer of cribs, car seats, strollers, and toys. Distributors and retailers were unflaggingly loyal and stockholders supportive. The ads, with their tag line "BestBaby—Best for Your Baby!," were familiar elements in parenting magazines. Product reviews were generally good, and the media were friendly. Although overall sales had remained relatively flat during the past few years, the company had been buoyed by strong sales from a recent line of collapsible jogging strollers introduced in 1997 and regularly updated with trendy colors like raspberry, blueberry, and tangerine.

What about consumers? "We haven't had more than the usual number of consumer complaints, especially after we instituted that satisfaction guarantee and five-year warranty a few years ago," Greg mused. Of course, the last few years had also produced their share of management challenges. There was that painful moment in November 1998 when Greg had had to order those cost-cutting measures. He'd had to lay off dozens of part-time workers and offer early retirement to more than a few full-time ones. He'd worked closely then with the new COO, Keith Sigismund, to streamline and consolidate BestBaby's supply chain. Following the winnowing process, one particular supplier, Arzep Enterprises, emerged as the chief provider of materials, furnishing BestBaby with 80% of its plastic, rubber, and metal parts; nylon cords; and other equipment.

Keith had proven himself serious, hardworking, and wholly dedicated, although his authoritarian, no-nonsense manner occasionally rankled managers and employees, especially those who worked in the manufacturing facility. Lisa Ronell, a popular, good-humored woman who headed up human resources, had fielded several complaints about Keith's apparent obliviousness to the shop-floor and warehouse personnel. During a meeting with Greg early last year, Lisa mentioned that one employee in particular—outspoken Donna Di Meola, who wore "Union: Yes!" buttons—had complained that Keith routinely ignored her when issues came up.

"Donna says that Keith doesn't really listen to her," Lisa had told Greg. "She says he's obviously preoccupied and cuts her off if she brings problems to his attention. I suggested that if that's the case, she should write up her communications as memos and bring issues to his attention that way. And keep copies." During Keith's last performance evaluation, Greg had urged him to brush up on his listening skills, without specifically mentioning Donna's complaints.

Suddenly, Greg also remembered Keith's saying that Arzep had recently switched suppliers, going with cheaper materials in an effort to shave expenses of its own. "Keith said that the new material isn't as sturdy as the previous brand, but he's never reported a diminishment in quality," Greg thought.

He resumed his mental inventory of corporate difficulties. "The only real mark against us was that liability suit six years ago, which we settled," he said to himself. "After that, I hired Robert Howe as corporate counsel. Boy, Robert did a great job on that stroller case last year, when he showed that our product didn't fail and that the nanny hadn't fastened the seat belt."

Point the Finger?

As the crisis meeting convened, Jane placed copies of the latest news clippings before each place at the conference table. Lisa pulled Greg aside as the senior managers found their seats. "Greg, I've had several people call this morning, wanting to see me," she worried. "Two managers in manufacturing told me they want to quit. So does Donna."

Greg nodded, taking in the bad news. "Lisa, do your best to keep people calm. Beg them not to quit. I'm planning on making a speech to the company after our meeting. Please ask them to hang on at least until the end of the day. And tell Donna I want to meet with her as soon as possible."

"Sure, Greg, I'll try," Lisa responded grimly. "But this whole Nelkin thing has really upset her. The only person around here who can do any persuading is you."

Lips tight, Greg moved to his place at the head of the conference table and cleared his throat. "Good morning. First things first: there's been no update on the condition of Avery Nelkin," Greg announced to the group. "I know you share my concern about this child. Of course, we all know we make a great product, but we're facing a real public relations crisis here. We have not yet answered calls from the media, but I agree with Jane that we should make some kind of announcement, and soon. So before we leave this room, we need to have a complete disclosure of everything we know about this issue," Greg waved his pile of clippings, "and a plan of action. Jane, you start by filling us in on the news reports."

Jane stood up. "Well, I'm assuming you all watched the news last night." She looked around the table, and several heads nodded. "Nelkin told reporters that his 14-year-old daughter, Sophie, was taking the baby out for a late-afternoon jog. Sophie claimed to have set the brake on the stroller while it was in the driveway. Then she went back to the house to lock the door, but while she was doing that, the stroller rolled down the driveway and fell on its side, and the baby's head hit the concrete." Jane paused. "So she called 911—that's the phone call all the radio stations keep playing. No one claims to have seen the incident, but Nelkin insists that this accident is not Sophie's fault. He says, quote, 'She's absolutely trustworthy and responsible, and this incident has traumatized her. It's clear that the brake on the stroller didn't work.'"

Keith sat through Jane's summary with a scowl on his face. When she was finished, he stood up and pulled what looked like a copy of a memo from his leather notebook. "I don't remember reading this at the time it was written, and I couldn't find it in any file, but Donna handed this to me this morning," he said grimly. "She's that union organizer in machining who likes to send me alarming memos on a weekly basis. I usually look into them, but so far they haven't unearthed any serious problems.

"Anyway, Donna told me this morning that she keeps copies of all her memos. This one is dated January 15, 2000." Keith cleared his throat and read aloud: "New Arzep brake fittings don't grab the front wheels as easily as previous ones. If the brakes actually fail, a child in the stroller could be hurt."

Everyone in the conference room gasped in unison. Simon Levison was visibly angry. He pounded his fist on the table. "Well, if that's true, then this is absolutely not our fault!" he fumed. "The problem is with Arzep's brake fittings, not our manufacturing. We can't be held responsible. I think we should put out a press release saying that we are looking into problems at Arzep."

Greg shook his head. "Simon, any kind of denial of the charges will certainly make things look worse. Besides," he pointed out, "if this memo has been leaked

outside the company, it will look like a smoking gun."
An uncomfortable silence fell over the room.

"Well, I definitely think we should issue a press release saying that we are investigating this matter, but we have to do more than that," said Jane finally.

"We have a great product. But in cases like this, the public has already determined our company's guilt because of the celebrity of the victim."

"Greg, you're going to have to go on TV and give some kind of profuse and public apology to Nick Nelkin, Celia Winston, and their family."

"He should absolutely do no such thing," snapped the lawyer, Robert Howe. He stared hard at Jane, who shifted uncomfortably. "No one saw the accident, and this very well could have been the teenager's fault. An apology will look like an admission of guilt."

Keith spoke up. "We have a great product and an airtight reason for pursuing Arzep. But in cases like this," he added with audible bitterness, "the public has already determined our company's guilt because of the celebrity of the victim."

Jane insisted that the company's chief concern at this moment was how to spin the story. "The public's memory is short," she said. "Is there any way we can undertake a totally separate PR campaign in a few months, to clean up the company's image? There may be an opportunity in this, depending on how we handle it. Maybe if we do some pro bono work and get the word out, in six months we'll look like Mother Teresa."

"Well, one thing is certain," said Greg. "This negative publicity is highly damaging and needs to be nipped in the bud. We have to be very careful in communicating with everyone—our own employees, the news media, the public, and the Nelkin family." He searched the faces at the table.

How Can BestBaby Bring Its PR Crisis Under Control?

Four commentators offer their advice.

➤ John R. Hall

John R. Hall is the retired chairman of Ashland Incorporated in Covington, Kentucky. As chairman from 1981 to 1997, he presided over his company's response when an Ashland storage tank collapsed in January 1988, spilling diesel fuel into the Monongahela and Ohio Rivers.

As a former CEO who went through a similarly harrowing experience, I can certainly sympathize with Greg James. Like him, I received a lot of conflicting advice from different people within my organization, yet I had to make the right decision for everyone, both inside and outside the company. And like Greg, I had to deal with some very unpleasant facts about which I was previously unaware. In the case of Ashland's 1988 oil spill, I learned to my horror that the storage tank that had collapsed was not a new model but a "recycled" one. To make matters worse, the engineers who had reconstructed the used tank had failed to pay sufficient attention to standard industry procedures.

Although it's possible that the incident involving the Nelkin baby was truly an accident, Greg has to assume that it wasn't, because that is the public's perception. Nor is it constructive to lay blame on anyone. Only by holding his company fully responsible can Greg ultimately restore the public's faith in BestBaby.

In Ashland's case, we reclaimed our good name as a corporate citizen by acting quickly and decisively to disclose all the facts, engage an outside investigator, and pay whatever price was necessary to clean up the mess. The price we paid for the cleanup was, in the end, money well spent. As a result of our aggressive actions, the press articles following the terrible incident were largely positive.

Greg should call a news conference as rapidly as possible. In it, he should apologize to the Nelkin family for any deficiency that may have existed in the stroller. He should offer the family his and the company's best wishes for their daughter's speedy and complete recovery. And he should announce a series of decisive actions. He should say that, as a first order of business, BestBaby will immediately recall all strollers of this type for investigation and possible modification of the brakes.

Second, Greg should openly state all the facts—including the change of suppliers and the warning memo from an employee—because leaving them for a reporter to discover later will be extremely damaging. In addition, he must say that the company is appointing a reputable, independent outside investigator to conduct a full review of the accident; he must promise that the conclusions of the investigation will be made public upon its completion. The investigation should include an evaluation of materials provided by all component suppliers. This is particularly important since BestBaby had made changes to its supply chain and since the change to new materials had been questioned by at least one employee. Once the study is complete, BestBaby should make it available to the baby stroller industry at large so that all companies involved in the manufacture of strollers might benefit from it. Finally, Greg should pledge full cooperation with all interested parties, including government agencies, the media, and the company's customers and suppliers.

During this press conference and subsequent statements, Greg should emphasize BestBaby's long history as a supplier of products for children and the company's reputation for superior product quality. He should clearly state his determination to find the exact cause of the problem and to modify the stroller to be certain that a similar incident will never occur. And finally, of course, BestBaby must deliver on all of Greg's promises, down to the finest detail. By doing all these things, it is entirely possible for Greg's company to emerge stronger and healthier.

➢ Ian Mitroff

Ian Mitroff is the Harold Quinton Distinguished Professor of Business Policy at the University of Southern California's Marshall School of Business. He is also the president of Comprehensive Crisis Management, a consulting firm in Manhattan Beach, California. His latest book is Managing Crises Before They Happen *(Amacom, 2000) with Gus Anagnos.*

This is not just a public relations crisis; it's a management crisis. The earlier lawsuits and the memos from Donna signaled the existence of ongoing problems at the company. The fact that Greg, Keith, and other executives ignored or minimized these early warning signs shows just how short-sighted BestBaby is. Had an effective crisis-management team been in place to pay attention to these signs, the current situation might have been avoided.

Unfortunately, the question of liability is already moot. Even if Robert, the attorney, were able to prove in a court of law that BestBaby isn't at fault, he's already lost the bigger, much more important case. In the emotionally volatile court of public opinion, a baby's injuries are the only admissible evidence, and there is no defense. Any attempt to deflect responsibility—as we have seen so clearly in the recent Ford and Firestone debacle—will only sink BestBaby more deeply into the quagmire. Nor should Greg blame anyone within the company. Rather, he will need to ask himself: what illness existed within our corporate structure that allowed this to happen? To treat the illness, BestBaby will have to swallow bitter medicine.

Besides bracing for a class action suit, Greg must now face the hard fact that he has only one real choice. He can pay once now for his company's mistakes or pay for them later on an ongoing basis. If he pays now, he has a much stronger chance of controlling the damage and reviving the company's public image. Therefore, like it or not, BestBaby must assume complete and total responsibility for the Nelkin accident and all others involving its products.

Greg's first task must be to find out the awful truth about unreported and unheeded product and supply problems before the media do. He should immediately hire an independent investigator to interview Donna and other employees privately and confidentially. The investigator will have to unearth the history of any problems and report all findings directly to Greg on a daily basis. Greg will also want to hire a crisis management expert who will be charged with setting up and training a permanent, internal crisis-management team comprising people from the operations, marketing, IT, security, and legal departments. The team will need to meet regularly with employees and report on and address issues on a monthly basis. Greg should definitely consider assigning Donna to the team.

At the press conference, Greg will have to cross his personal Rubicon. He will have to look right into the cameras and say, "We violated the trust of consumers." He must be absolutely sincere and contrite. He must make a frank apology to the Nelkins and anyone else whose children have been injured by BestBaby products, and he must offer to pay all their medical expenses. He must truthfully lay out all the facts as he understands them. Greg keeps an upper hand only by airing the facts on his terms; he can be sure that, if they haven't already, the media will find out about Donna's memo. He must also lay out an aggressive plan of action, detailing how and when his company will fix organizational and operational problems. He should introduce the members of his new crisis-management team. And he must schedule another press conference in three days to update the public.

In the following months and years, BestBaby will have to repair its public image by consistently demonstrating to the media and the public how the company has redefined itself. Executive management should review all company business practices and key assumptions and reject or revise those that have brought BestBaby to this pass. The company should open its facilities to inspection, showing how it has changed its operations for the better. Greg and his staff will need to think outside the business-as-usual box and identify with children and parents. They will have to make amends through some highly visible, charitable acts to prove that BestBaby can rise to an ethical standard far beyond that of the bottom line.

➤ Robin Cohn

Robin Cohn is a New York–based crisis-management consultant and the author of The PR Crisis Bible *(St. Martin's, 2000). She directed the response of Air Florida after the fatal crash of its Flight 90 in the Potomac River in 1982.*

Greg and Jane are correct in wanting to get out a media statement, but they have waited too long already. In the early stages of a crisis, the faster the story is out, the more quickly it can be contained and the more forgiving the public is willing to be. The crisis meeting should have been called as soon as the company heard about the accident, and Greg should have issued a statement that same evening.

The minute this meeting is over, Greg should personally call the Nelkin family. He should offer to meet with them privately and to provide whatever assistance possible, including paying the medical bills. Such a meeting should not be publicized. Then Greg should issue a voluntary recall before the U.S. Consumer Product Safety Commission asks for one. He should require the company's distributors to stop selling jogging strollers until further notice. He and Keith should also apologize to Donna.

With these orders of business out of the way, Greg should address the employees. His statement can serve as a rehearsal for the public one. He should say something like: "I know all of you are shocked by the Nelkin baby accident. We've always prided ourselves on making the best equipment, yet something here went terribly wrong, and we have to fix it immediately. I am about to hold a press conference. On behalf of all of us, I will apologize to the Nelkin family as well as to our other customers. I will announce a product recall; I will also stress that we are developing new quality-control procedures to see that this never happens again. We will be discussing these steps with you before releasing them to the media." Greg should also tell the staff that Donna tried to alert management about the problem and that he has apologized to her.

Greg's statement to the media will have to accomplish several simultaneous objectives. It's important to stress his company's concern for its customers and to show that it has nothing to hide. He should not assign blame. The public does not care about what's legally acceptable. It cares only about what's morally acceptable, which is that Best-Baby is responsible for the safety of its products. If the company appears to deny responsibility, respond too slowly, cover up, or put its own interests first, the public will lash out—and damage to BestBaby's reputation could be irreparable.

Aside from expressing sincere concern for the Nelkin baby and other children injured in stroller accidents, Greg will have to state all the facts as he knows them. He won't have complete information at the time of the press conference, so he should say that the company is working to determine the cause of the accident and to fix it and that BestBaby will continue to provide information as it becomes available. He should add that the company is voluntarily recalling its jogging strollers and stress that it will work with the Consumer Product Safety Commission. Finally, he should introduce Jane Benson as the future spokesperson. It will be Jane's unenviable job to make absolutely sure that the public stays apprised of the results of the investigation.

Greg should open up the floor to the tough questions that reporters will ask and address each one as candidly as he can. If, for example, someone mentions the employee memo, Greg will have to admit its oversight and emphasize that the company is investigating the matter. If questions arise about the brakes, he should not yet mention Arzep's name since the cause of the accident, although suspected, has not been determined.

Unfortunately, even the most deftly conducted press conferences are not enough to begin rebuilding customer loyalty. This can only be accomplished one consumer at a time. BestBaby will have to surpass public expectations. Greg should ask himself: "If I owned a jogging stroller like this, what's the most fair and generous thing BestBaby could do for me?" The company might, for example, replace the recalled strollers with top-of-the-line models. Certainly, such replacements would come at a substantial cost. But a response like this would go a long way toward heading off public anger—and, in the end, cost far less than the price the company would pay for belated action or additional inaction.

➤ Alan H. Schoem

Alan H. Schoem is the director of the Office of Compliance of the U.S. Consumer Product Safety Commission in Washington, DC.

BestBaby is in trouble, but its situation is not hopeless. The most effective way for the company to address its defective brake problem and restore consumer confidence in its name is to work cooperatively with the U.S. Consumer Product Safety Commission (CPSC; www.cpsc.gov) to recall its jogging strollers. If the company acts quickly in mounting a recall, it can demonstrate its commitment to its customers and to product safety.

In this unfortunate event, BestBaby even has a role model. On October 4, 1982, Johnson & Johnson announced a nationwide recall of 31 million bottles of Tylenol after seven people died from taking cyanide-laced Extra Strength Tylenol capsules. It was one of the most prominent product recalls in the United States, and the company's aggressive action went a long way toward restoring trust in its brand. In the end, Tylenol more than survived; Johnson & Johnson also raised the standard for consumer product packaging.

Greg and BestBaby will have to accept the fact that they are likely to be sued by Nelkin and others. The company should not allow that likelihood to interfere with its recall. Its goal should be to prevent other injuries or potential deaths. And it would serve BestBaby no useful purpose to blame its supplier for the problem. In the public's mind, BestBaby is responsible since it manufactures the strollers. Legal action against Arzep can always be pursued later.

BestBaby should immediately contact the CPSC's Office of Compliance and ask for help in conducting a recall under our Fast Track Product Recall Program. Under it, a company reports its problem to the CPSC and offers to conduct a recall. In exchange for this cooperation, the CPSC foregoes conducting a detailed evaluation of the product and making a preliminary determination that the item possesses a defect and is a substantial product hazard.

The company has a lot to do in a very short time. To avoid the commission staff's making a preliminary determination of hazard, BestBaby must initiate its recall within 20 working days. Issuing a recall requires more than simply sending out a press release; for the recall to be effective and acceptable to the CPSC, it must follow the specifications of the Fast Track program. Thus, before the official recall can begin, BestBaby must first work with the CPSC to determine the scope of the recall by pinpointing exactly when Arzep changed the brake components; perhaps the recall can be limited to those strollers with inferior brakes. Second, BestBaby must determine the remedy it will make available to customers. Repairing and eliminating the brake problem would likely be the least expensive option. If a repair is not immediately available, the company could offer a refund of the purchase price or a replacement stroller.

Once the remedy is agreed upon, BestBaby must work with the CPSC to figure out the most effective ways to notify consumers of its efforts to remove the dangerous strollers from the marketplace. The company can also use this public notice to alleviate some of the negative publicity surrounding its product and the accident involving baby Nelkin. Greg might also wish to participate in the CPSC's press conference announcing this recall and to issue a joint press release with the CPSC. Because of the very real risk of serious injury and death as well as the negative publicity surrounding the company, BestBaby also would do well to announce the recall in paid advertisements. While the CPSC does not allow ads announcing a recall to be marketing tools, the agency would allow language expressing the company's commitment to its customers. BestBaby must also post the recall notice prominently on its Web site and place recall posters in retail stores that sold the strollers and in pediatricians' offices.

In the CPSC's experience, companies that are up-front with their customers—and that act quickly to prevent further injuries—can maintain or regain the loyalty and admiration of the public.

The comments by Mr. Schoem were made in his official capacity and are in the public domain; they do not necessarily reflect the position of the CPSC.

Originally published in April 2001

Reprint R0104A

PAUL F. NUNES AND BRIAN A. JOHNSON

Are Some Customers More Equal Than Others?

Executive Summary

Jill Hoover was looking skyward, marveling at the heart-stopping beauty of Paradise Park–Seattle's newest attraction, its tallest and scariest roller coaster to date: the Anaconda. "Quite impressive," Jill thought. But a scuffle in the ride queue quickly brought the CEO of Paradise Parks back to earth.

The company's 19 seasonal and year-round amusement parks had always been popular—ever since Jill's father founded the original Paradise Park just after the Second World War—but they hadn't been very profitable of late. Operating costs had been spiraling, and every dollar of extra revenue had been hard won. At the company's annual management off-site

Executive Summary

meeting, held that morning at the Seattle park, CFO
Nathan Cortland proposed that Paradise offer its customers the option of a "preferred guest" card. Cardholders would pay more, but they would get first
crack at the rides—entering through separate lines—
and would get seated immediately at any of the
parks' restaurants. According to Nathan, the plan
would bolster Paradise's sagging finances because it
would target the "mass affluents"—a rising demographic of moneyed but time-pressed people who
might visit the park more often and spend more if it
weren't for long lines at the rides.

Jill respects Nathan's idea—but hasn't her plan to
upgrade some of the parks' souvenir shops to gift
boutiques already shown some promise? And doesn't
Nathan's plan smack of elitism, as Jill's longtime
friend and fellow park manager Adam Goodwin suggests? The CEO has resolved to get back to Nathan
with a decision about "Operation Upmarket" by the
time she leaves Seattle and returns to headquarters.
Should Paradise Parks offer guests different levels of
service? Four commentators offer their advice in this
fictional case study.

Jill Hoover grinned as the sound of children's screams filled the air around her. "Could you please repeat that, Bill?" she called out to the park manager, who was explaining the sophisticated safety features of the roller coaster they were walking toward. Jill was getting her first look at the Anaconda, the newest—and biggest—attraction in the group of theme parks her company ran nationwide. She had seen the ride in various stages of development, but the final product was truly something to behold, especially in action. "It's incredible!" she marveled, as much to herself as to her CFO, Nathan Cortland, who had just caught up to the tour. But the moment soured as she noticed a scuffle in the long line of people waiting to ride. A couple of tough kids—young men, really—had tried to jump the queue, and other people weren't standing for it. Bill was already moving toward them and murmuring into his walkie-talkie: "Security to the Anaconda, code 3."

Nathan jumped on the opportunity to score a point. "See? This is what I mean," he said. "Some people just can't deal with lines. Give 'em the option not to, and you'd be surprised what it's worth to 'em."

"You think so, huh?" Jill shot back. "Do those two strike you as the 'mass affluents' we should be targeting?" It was a small-minded retort, she knew, and not becoming of the president and CEO of Paradise Parks. But honestly, she was already tired of Nathan's con-

---

The top 20% of U.S. incomes now accounted for more than 48% of total entertainment spending; Paradise wanted a share of that pie.

---

stant drumbeating for his proposed Operation Upmarket. It was three months ago that he had first approached her with the idea of a "preferred guest card" as a way to win more business from an increasingly moneyed—but time-pressed—group of people that the folks in market research referred to as "mass affluents." Nathan had learned that the top 20% of U.S. incomes now accounted for more than 48% of total U.S. spending on entertainment fees and admissions, and he intended to get Paradise Parks' share of that pie. Under his plan, visitors could pay an additional fee to get free rein of the park: Cardholders would enter the rides through separate lines that would give them first crack, and they would be seated immediately at any in-park restaurant.

At first blush, Jill hadn't liked the sound of this preferential treatment. But she respected Nathan's judgment; he had been her father's right-hand man for years. So she had asked him to present the idea at the annual management off-site, which was always held at one of the company's parks. This year, it was being held here at Paradise Park–Seattle, to celebrate the opening of the company's tallest roller coaster ever.

For his part, Nathan had done an impressive amount of work developing the idea, commissioning surveys and focus groups, and getting finance to run the numbers on all kinds of pricing permutations. His chance to unveil Operation Upmarket had finally come that morning, and Jill had to admit that his presentation had been persuasive, even with his not-so-subtle facilitation of the discussion. His tactic had been to get people arguing the details—Should the pass cost $20 more than general admission, or $30 more?— while brushing right past the question of whether it was a good idea at all. At first, this approach seemed to be working.

In the Beginning

It was Paradise's vice president of human resources who eventually derailed the debate. "Clearly, there's revenue to be gained from offering these differentiated service levels," she said. "But—oh, I don't know—it just doesn't seem like us. You know . . . our whole tradition, our culture." No one in the room needed her to elaborate. Paradise Parks was created by a man they all had worked with until his death five years earlier—a man they revered without exception.

Francis "Fritz" Hoover was born in 1920, a child of the Depression, and had grown up just fast enough to see fighting in two theaters of World War II. The experience forged his strong belief that people were at their best when circumstances forced them to set aside their differences. He had fought side by side with men of various classes and races; any prejudices he might have held were left behind on the battlefield. The fact that so many soldiers had done the same, he often said, was the real victory of the war. When his tour of duty was over, no one in his family was surprised at his choice of occupation. Fritz used a GI loan to buy a small seasonal fair outside of Milwaukee. He quickly reorganized its attractions around a variety of themes that expressed his vision of idyllic American life—Townsquare, Frontierworld, Playland, and so on—and renamed it Paradise Park. The idea was to create a place where families could come together for a day to forget about their cares, a place where people could enjoy their shared humanity, in an environment that highlighted the best of human endeavors.

With a postwar baby boom in full swing, Paradise Park became an instant success. Eventually, Fritz opened five Paradise Parks, all in secondary urban markets like the one he grew up in. This choice had the added benefit of keeping real-estate prices low. While larger competitors had gone on to become "destination sites," Fritz preferred to keep his parks—and investments—relatively small, having never forgotten the bank failures of his youth. Paradise Parks were intended to serve markets of roughly four million to 15 million people living within three hours' drive of the sites (approximately 150 miles).

When business slowed in the 1980s, Fritz followed his competitors' moves into niche parks, including water parks and syndicated-cartoon theme parks. Paradise held the advantage here because it had always served smaller locales with an entertainment option that was considered good value. The beginnings of an echo boom in the 1990s helped business, and over time, Paradise was lured into expanding its business into undeveloped neighboring land and experimenting with destination roller coasters, water rides, and theatrical performances. These moves helped the business but had required significant investments.

By the time Jill took over as CEO, Paradise owned and operated 19 seasonal and year-round amusement parks, all within the United States, seven of them full-blown Paradise Parks. Annual attendance varied—from more than five million at the largest, most popular park to 300,000 at the smallest one. Overall attendance now slightly exceeded 23 million people, a number Jill found awe inspiring considering where they had begun.

Trouble in Paradise

But if everyone at the off-site meeting knew about the company's roots, they were even more acutely aware of its current situation. Nathan summarized their thoughts during his presentation: "Our history is great, but if things don't turn around fast, we're going to *be* history." For all the growth and excitement of the past two decades, profits had remained slim. Labor costs had skyrocketed with the low unemployment of the late 1990s, and insurance rates had soared after a series of industry mishaps. Along with those market factors, the capital costs of building the new rides that Paradise thought it needed to compete in today's market were rising, and the real-estate tax benefits it had received when the parks were originally built (awarded for creating jobs in the locations chosen) were expiring. Finally, it happened: Paradise had its first money-losing year, followed by another. And, as Nathan correctly pointed out, the company would have to make changes quickly to avoid a cash-crunch-driven bankruptcy or a hostile takeover—both of which threatened to ruin Fritz's dream.

It was no secret that theme parks had only three ways to bring in more revenue: increase visits per customer, increase average spending per visit, or attract new customers. The industry's maturity made all three hard to do. Parks typically use discounts to increase visits per customer—in a recent promotion, for example, Paradise Parks had printed $10-off coupons on 15 million soda cans. But while the added attendance from the coupons had increased the parks' profits from in-park spending, those were largely offset by a loss in gate receipts. Paradise Parks' in-park spending per customer had grown significantly over time but was now stalled near $35, a level that would be hard to surpass without significant innovation. And unless Paradise could pull in people from a broader geographic area—an unlikely proposition given the wide availability of theme parks—attracting more customers would require that the company create new value propositions. Nathan claimed that Operation Upmarket would address the last two goals: "Clearly, this plan is a way to up-sell the people who are already coming to the park. And, by making it possible to spend less time in queues, the guest card will also attract a different type of customer—time-starved, high-income professionals and their families, who might otherwise avoid the whole experience."

But Jill had her own ideas about how to tap into that affluent segment. In fact, she had already spearheaded some successes. Roughly 20% of Paradise Parks' souvenir shops had been upgraded to gift boutiques, with more appealing displays and higher-priced merchandise. A similar shift was under way to convert some snack concessions to seated dining. The most up-scale of the restaurants were already earning almost double the profit per square foot of the other food-service facilities. Jill had also recruited a new head of business development to attract more conference business—although, she noted, he was the quickest to support Nathan's idea. "This is terrific," he had enthused. "Conference organizers are always looking for perks for their attendees. They'll eat this up."

"Okay," Jill cut in; the meeting had begun to degenerate into side debates. "I think it's clear we're not going to make an immediate decision on this, but I did want you all to hear Nathan's proposal in detail. Let's keep talking about it over the days to come. It's been a long morning session, and I'm sure you're as excited as I am about lunch in our newest restaurant, Pêche Originale, followed by the Anaconda tour." The meeting was over, but the buzz continued as the group made its way out of the conference room.

The Ups and Downs

The day after the meeting and the Anaconda tour, Jill found herself strolling the grounds of another Paradise Park, experiencing the rush of memories this park always brought on. It was near the town where her parents had bought a summer home in the 1960s, and it was the scene of her youth—her first job, her first crush. The park was being managed now by Adam

Goodwin, whom she'd worked alongside way back when. They had spent countless hours together, ushering passengers onto the monorail, sweeping up litter, and hawking T-shirts.

"It strikes me as a very shortsighted strategy," Adam said, somewhat annoyed at management's consideration of the preferred guest program. Jill had decided to stop off on her way back from Seattle, ostensibly to see

---

"A couple of ugly glances, a nasty remark, and the day is spoiled for everybody. Neither side's coming back."

---

the park's new restaurants but mostly to sound out Adam. "I mean, sure we could make a lot of money on those cards in the first couple of seasons. But just think about what it does to the overall customer experience. The average Joe with his wife and three kids is not going to shell out for five upgrades. So they're going to be sweating through even longer lines and just steaming when they see some yuppie waltz ahead of them."

"Adam, let's be honest," Jill pushed back, "the long lines we're talking about aren't for the kiddie rides."

"Let me finish," Adam insisted. "I don't even think it's a great experience for the preferred guests. Who wants to feel all that animosity directed at them? I don't have to tell you, Jill, that the key to this business is the customers feeling good while they're here. A couple of ugly glances, a nasty remark, and the day is spoiled for everybody. Neither side's coming back."

"I should have explained," Jill countered. "We would definitely separate the lines so it wouldn't be in people's faces, and we'd limit the percentage of special tickets issued on any given day." She was amazed at how easily Nathan's arguments flowed from her lips. "But also, maybe you're not giving our customers enough credit. Maybe we need to acknowledge that this isn't the 1960s anymore. People have a lot more awareness and appreciation of the fact that time is money. This program lets them choose which they want to save more of."

Adam wasn't biting. "Look, this may be out of line, but I'll say it. I think it's an elitist program, and I don't think your father would have gone for it." He paused to let his words sink in and to let the chill they both felt settle.

When Jill spoke again, it took some effort to keep her voice steady. "Okay, I'm not crazy about it, either. But it's crunch time. If we don't do this, we might have to raise prices across the board. Is that better or worse for the average customer? I hear everything you're saying, but I need to make Paradise profitable so we can hold on to it. At the end of the day, that's what Dad would want."

They turned the corner past a group of kids buying sno-cones and found themselves by the stairs to the monorail. "Hey, how long has it been since you rode this?" Adam asked, conciliatory now.

Jill looked up and managed a smile. "And how about that: No line. C'mon. Bet I can remember the script better than you."

Heading home that night, Jill was relieved to spot an open desk near the window in the airline's first-class lounge. A flight cancellation at a nearby gate had made the hallway just outside the room chaotic, but as the lounge's thick mahogany door closed behind her, classical music replaced the travelers' din. She settled into a leather chair as a steward passed by, calling her attention to the fruit buffet he had just replenished.

Nathan had asked for her thoughts following the off-site meeting; given the systems and other infrastructure required to implement his plan, work would have to begin soon to have it ready for the following season. Jill resolved to devote tonight's flight time to enumerating the pros and cons, and her goal was to have a memo to Nathan drafted by the time she reached Milwaukee.

Would Nathan's plan to create a new class of preferred customers enhance Paradise Parks' performance or undermine it? That was the essential question. With 20 minutes to spare until boarding time, she glanced toward the buffet. While her thoughts continued to race, she couldn't help but notice how unusual it was for the airline club to be serving fresh figs—and how tempting they looked.

Should Paradise Offer Different Levels of Service?

Four commentators offer expert advice.

➤ John Harrington

John Harrington is CEO of the Boston Red Sox.

Boy, do I identify with Jill Hoover and the decision she's trying to make. For 30 years, I've been involved in a business—baseball—that's even more associated with democratic ideals than hers and in a town that takes such ideals very seriously.

The Boston Red Sox has been a family business, owned by Tom and Jean Yawkey since 1933, and I have been privileged to be treated like a member of that family. Since becoming CEO of the organization—and even before that, as treasurer—I've thought constantly about how they would have approached the decisions I've had to make as the dynamics of this business have changed.

The sad fact is that Tom Yawkey, had he not been diagnosed with cancer in 1975, probably would not have lasted in baseball anyway. That was the year free agency entered the game and forever changed the nature of the business. Tom had run the club as a sort of gentleman's hobby; he was in it for the personal satisfaction of fielding competitive teams, not to turn a profit. He would have been dismayed to hear that the average salary of the players in the industry is now $2 million. Back then, it was about $55,000.

Player salaries now represent 65% of our costs. So as those costs began to skyrocket, there was no question that we had to raise new revenue. To do that, we increasingly focused on the customers who were willing to pay more. We put in luxury suites along the roof, for example, and created our "600 Club"—a comfortably enclosed seating area right behind home plate, staffed with waiters serving fare not available in the bleachers. The new ballpark that we're proposing to build goes even further to accommodate big spenders.

At every turn, we've been aware of the elitism we're displaying—and we're concerned about the bleacher fan's reaction. To counter any ill will, we've always tried to point out that the revenue we are raising allows us to keep the lowest-priced bleacher seats as cheap as possible. And in fact, while the per-seat, per-game cost of a suite has now reached $130, it is still possible to get in the door for $9— not to see the Red Sox take on the Yankees, granted, but when a less competitive team is in town.

Even if there hadn't been such a huge increase in payroll costs, we still would have gone with the plan to offer an enhanced experience to premium customers. It's a function of how the entertainment environment has changed. Once people decide to spend the time on an activity, they are happy to spend the extra dollar for an even better time. At the ticket windows, for instance, we've found that 75% of fans will ask for a box seat before accepting a lower-priced one. And despite the fact that Red Sox ticket prices are the second highest in the league, our total attendance figures in 2001 set another record for Fenway Park.

It's a no-brainer—Jill needs to target those customers who will pay more for a better experience. But rather than proceed ad hoc with her CFO's suggestion—offering a preferred guest card—Jill should craft a master plan of all the ways the park will attract an increasing number of premium customers. She should also consider other nontraditional sources of revenue—for instance, corporate sponsorships and advertising.

Will Jill have to wrestle with her conscience to do this? No doubt. I remember the day I accompanied the Yawkeys to a season opener where they got their first look at our new electronic scoreboard—flanked by advertisements from Marlboro, Gillette, and Budweiser. The Yawkeys were horrified, and that bothered me. But our revenue-producing moves have sustained the competitive team that Tom Yawkey took such pride in. We haven't won the World Series in a long while, but since free agency came along, the Red Sox have produced the second-best win-loss record in baseball.

And as for the World Series—we'll take it next year.

➤ Edward Goldman

Edward Goldman is a cofounder of MDVIP, a premium health-care service based in Florida.

Creating two tiers of service at different prices will create problems for Jill, and she's right to hesitate to do it. Why not just raise the admission price across the board? And while she's at it, she might bring the prices at Paradise Parks' restaurants and gift shops up another notch, too. If her CFO is right about the growth of a new demographic class of mass affluents, then this kind of price increase will work. These people will self-select into a park that offers faster lines and tonier goods and services. Attendance will dip—indeed, that's the point—but overall revenues will rise.

It may be a controversial decision among Jill and her senior managers, but her actions will hardly attract the broader political scrutiny that my partners and I did when we made an analogous move.

Our business, MDVIP, came about because a few physicians in Boca Raton, Florida, were frustrated with a health-care reimbursement system that encouraged them to take on heavy patient caseloads. It's a widespread phenomenon that has resulted in average doctor-patient consultations across the industry of less than ten minutes—and long waits to get those appointments. Our solution was to reduce the size of the practice from 3,000 patients to a maximum of 600 and to charge those patients an annual fee of

$1,500. Thus, without losing any revenue, physicians have time to spend on the preventive care, like annual physicals, that Medicare, for example, does not cover. Most important, the physicians can offer nearly immediate service—or, in Jill's terms, "no lines."

Any time you introduce change to the health-care arena, there is controversy, and we are taking some heat. For instance, our own Florida senator, Bill Nelson, has expressed a fear of the systemwide effects that would be felt if physicians were to move to this kind of structure en masse—a scenario that I consider highly unlikely. We would have encountered far more resistance had we chosen to provide two different tiers of service within a practice. That would have created a situation in which the person who went to the head of the line would not necessarily be the person who had the most acute medical problem—an idea that is morally repugnant.

In the case of an amusement park, the implications are obviously less dire. Over time, people might come to accept the differentiation. For instance, I am amazed at how people in airports will watch passively as first-class customers board the plane ahead of them, even after they've suffered through multihour delays. Still, in that situation, there is no dramatic difference in the service—the plane leaves the gate at the same time for all and is just as well maintained. There would be more of an uproar if there were a serious gap in quality or safety.

The question for Paradise Parks is, How much does the increased wait in line for the average customer represent a degradation in the quality of the park visit? I can only say that for us the value of time is paramount. Our practice aims for an impact on convenience rather than on quality of care, and we succeed to the extent that 90% of our patients who call are seen the same day. Convenience has a greater value for some people than for others. We priced our product at $1,500 to keep it within the range of the busy individual who is not necessarily rich.

Would I have a strong sense of moral indignation if Paradise Parks offered two tiers of service? No. America is still a place where people can make money and spend it the way they want. I'm a great believer in market forces. But I don't think the market would reward Paradise Parks for placing some gold-card-carrying exclusive club alongside its basic customers. Take a doctor's advice: Raise the gate prices. It will lower everyone's blood pressure.

➤ Alexander Labak

Alexander Labak is chief marketing officer at Deutsche Bank in Frankfurt, Germany.

In my company, Deutsche Bank, we recently addressed the question Jill is facing, but we had none of her qualms about it. For us, it simply made good business sense to segment our customers and to offer a different level of service—at a higher price—to those at the upper end of the market. This strategy would work for Paradise Parks, as well. The key is to do it discreetly and in a way that does not degrade the quality of service to the basic customer.

The discretion I'm urging should take several forms. Obviously, the expedited line should be hidden from the view of those waiting in a longer one. But also, the preferred guest program should be designed as a bundle of services—including things like premium seating for in-park entertainment or "backstage passes" for cardholders and their families—so that its whole focus is not something as galling as line jumping.

Meanwhile, in its marketing efforts, Paradise Parks must not make the program seem exclusionary—that certain customers are not welcome to participate in it. Instead, the company should present the program as a rational response to varying customer needs. This was certainly the approach we took at Deutsche Bank when we realigned our business into Private Banking services and Deutsche Bank 24 services. The former services are for the upper end of the market, and the bank offers highly tailored solutions for managing those clients' assets. The latter services offer most of the bank's customized products and services for standard customers. As we launched the services, we segmented our customer base and suggested to customers which direction might be most appropriate for them. There was some pushback from the press—a few journalists tried to paint an image of a bank consigning some customers to a lower class. But in general, it has not been hard for people to accept that customers with more money probably have more complicated needs related to managing their finances. Discretion in marketing the program means avoiding any elitist note and instead promoting the wisdom of "different strokes for different folks."

While implementing its premium service, Paradise Parks must ensure that the quality of service for standard customers doesn't drop to unsatisfactory levels. This will ensure that the cardholders themselves have no misgivings about the royal treatment they are being given—a fear of Adam's that I think is unfounded. In my experience, receiving premium service doesn't weigh on customers' consciences if they are *paying* more to receive that extra service.

Will the preferred guest program yield the increased revenues the park so badly needs? Probably, but Paradise should not count on attracting new customers—except perhaps through the conference business. What the program will do is help to retain prized customers, and it will increase average spending per customer. If I were the CFO of Paradise Parks, I would be ever mindful of the cost of such a large fixed-asset base and the need to keep the park full. I would aim for a balance by which the masses in general would cover my basic costs and my "preferred customers" would contribute the profits over and above that break-even point.

Indeed, it is hard for me to imagine the industry in which service differentiation would be inappropriate. Why wouldn't it make sense, for example, to extend this thinking even to a basic commodity like energy? While most customers will pay, say, $100 for basic service, a few customers might be willing to pay $500 for a guarantee of no blackouts. In a sense, the high-paying customer subsidizes the service to the standard customer.

Following a "one size fits all" strategy is, in most cases, a recipe for failure. If you try to meet everyone's needs with one level of service, you underserve everyone.

➤ Robert Crandall

Robert Crandall is a former chairman, president, and CEO of American Airlines. He currently serves on the boards of Anixter International, Celestica, Clear Channel Communications, Halliburton, and i2 Technologies.

Jill clearly has to act—she can't just keep losing money. She hasn't done the work needed to formulate a plan for Paradise Parks that will turn its finances around. As far as I can tell, she has no precise idea why the company is losing money. Are all the parks in trouble or only some of them? Are the losses coming from the big rides? The little rides? The restaurants and gift shops? Which are the most popular rides? Has Paradise carefully considered and measured the impact that its pricing policies, ride durations, and waiting times for rides have on customers? Jill will need all that information and lots more before she can come up with a sensible plan of action.

Moreover, Jill blew a great opportunity to use the off-site meeting to ask for and to explore alternative ideas. And she'll need them, because even if it does turn out that there is simply a generalized need for more revenue, the preferred-customer-card program probably isn't the right way to get it.

Customers just won't accept the kind of arrangement that CFO Nathan Cortland is advocating. The business will surely suffer if the average customer goes to the park and finds he can't get on the best rides because the place is full of conventioneers who are entitled to jump the line. That's not to say that people won't accept the concept of different accommodations at different prices; they're already used to that. But service differentiation at an amusement park must be subtler and far more sophisticated than what Nathan has proposed.

Paradise Parks could offer all its guests the opportunity to reserve a time slot for a particular ride. The parks might allocate a fixed number of seats to reservations—say a third or a half—and then give the folks lining up an option to wait or to make ride reservations for later in the day. That way, those who reserve and those who wait only have to live with their own—or their kids'—choices. Having taken that first step, Paradise might then want to experiment with other modifications that create added value for park guests. For example, it might be possible, without attracting adverse publicity, to offer those who stay at in-park hotels more ride and meal reservations per day than those who simply buy a general admission for the day. If this sort of approach is adopted, Paradise will need to establish a carefully structured tracking system. It would be important, for example, to know how many of those who stay at in-park hotels actually use the allocated reservations; that will indicate just how much value that particular component of the guest's visit adds to the room rate.

Whatever she decides to try, Jill should conduct beta tests in one of the parks. Focus groups are very useful, but people in such groups aren't always truthful; sometimes the truth is too ugly to divulge. For now, all she can reasonably do is outline her thinking about the profit problem: the changes in park operations that should be considered and the data that will be needed to implement those changes. Then, Jill should reconvene her senior management, spend some time picking everyone's brains, and finalize a program of experimentation likely to result in a successful package of new initiatives.

As for the case's soupy discussion of her father's ideals, it's simply irrelevant. Jill needs to remember that she's running a business. Her purpose is not to run theme parks, but to make money for shareholders. If it turns out that the best way to maximize Paradise Parks' value is to sell off the business for its real-estate value, that's what Jill should do. Come to think of it, Paradise Park would be a neat name for a gated community.

Originally published in November 2001

Reprint R0110A

License to Overkill

Executive Summary

Sheldon Bloomfield, senior vice president of character properties for Multi-Media Worldwide, has a hit with Baby Ruby. Originally a children's book character, Ruby has become the fastest-growing kids' show on television. And if negotiations with Galaxy Pictures go well, Baby Ruby might reach the big screen next summer. In fact, Sheldon's starting to wonder whether Baby Ruby is his evergreen property—the one that will generate licensing income for years to come.

Sheldon has to move carefully if he's going to make Baby Ruby's fame last longer than the proverbial 15 minutes. He's got many offers on the table,

Executive Summary

including one from the nation's leading fast-food franchiser to make Baby Ruby its next kids' meal tie-in. These deals would expand Baby Ruby's audience, but the terms are much less favorable than Sheldon would like. The fact is, no one wants to risk making a big financial commitment to a relatively new property, and most of the companies are demanding exclusives—which would eat away at Sheldon's profits even more.

The pressure is on. Sheldon knows if he doesn't make these deals, he may not get another chance. But if he does make the deals, and Baby Ruby ends up on everything from T-shirts to collectible spoons, the public may lose all interest in her.

Can Sheldon ensure that Baby Ruby becomes more than just the fast-food flavor of the month? Commentators Grant McCracken, a visiting scholar at McGill University and the author of *Culture and Consumption;* Jack Soden, CEO of Elvis Presley Enterprises; Timothy Rothwell, a senior vice president of Universal Studios Consumer Products Group; and Bill Griffith, creator of the comic strip *Zippy the Pinhead*, offer their advice in this fictional case study.

"Bill, it's Sheldon. You've got Ruby!"

Sitting by the pool of his Hollywood Hills home, Sheldon paused for effect. Although it was 8:30 AM in Chicago, it was still only 6:30 here in Los Angeles—a little early, he felt, to be nearly shouting into the phone.

"They all wanted her, but I said you had to have her. She's going to be big! Not like anything you've ever seen. She's got legs; this is just the beginning."

Sheldon Bloomfield, senior vice president of character properties for Multi-Media Worldwide, was delivering the news of the impending licensing deal with Quick & Good Burger to the fast-food giant's vice president of promotions and licensing, Bill Westman. Q&G's kids' meal promotion was *the* deal to get in restaurant tie-ins. Sheldon and Bill had been working on it for months, trying to make plush toys of MMW's property, *Baby Ruby*—the fastest-growing children's show on television—the next big kids' meal tie-in. After finally approving the terms of Q&G's most recent offer, Sheldon was hoping to hear some excitement in Bill's voice.

"That's great news," Bill replied, with guarded enthusiasm. "Does this mean she got the three-movie deal?"

Sheldon tried to keep the pause short while he fashioned his response. "Not exactly, Bill. Just one—but the studio won't do it without the option for two more. They're really excited. They know she's going to be bigger than King Lizards or Gooey People."

That wasn't what Bill wanted to hear, and Sheldon knew it. Hesitation on the studio's part could mean only one thing: concern about the longevity of Baby Ruby's appeal. The leading fast-food franchising chain, Quick & Good had no interest in associating with fly-by-night fads or low-profile characters. Q&G's size was enough to secure it the best properties from the top licensers in the world, whenever it came calling. And now it had come calling about Baby Ruby.

"That's too bad about the sequels, but I'm sure she'll do great." Bill paused. "We've got just a few more details to iron out on the proposal before we send you a final version next week. Sound good?"

Sheldon could feel his hair stand up on end. "A few more details" almost certainly meant Q&G intended to adjust the numbers downward. Somehow he managed to bellow an enthusiastic response. "Sounds great. My team will be waiting for it. I'm going to see you on the Vineyard in two weeks, right? Spectacular!"

Hanging up, Sheldon brought his towel to the edge of the pool and dived in. As he began his usual 50-lap routine, his mind drifted to how his odyssey with Baby Ruby had begun.

Yes Sir, That's My Baby

Sheldon had first laid eyes on Baby Ruby in a small bookstore in London. He had been in England on assignment, working on a number of international licensing deals for MMW, and had brought his wife and children with him. While he was browsing for interesting children's bedtime stories, his three-year-old daughter, Charlotte, had nearly pulled off his arm leading him to a book with a classic baby doll on the cover. Though he hadn't recognized it, she clearly knew it as Baby Ruby. "She's on the television here," his wife had explained. Sheldon had been far too busy to notice. Suddenly aware of how many times he had left his family's rental flat while the children were asleep and had returned when they were in bed again, he assuaged his guilt by buying every available Baby Ruby story—12 books in all.

Sheldon had managed a lot of children's characters in his time. In fact, he had made his career on them: buying the rights, selling the rights, trading the rights, and losing the rights. He had seen more than his share of cartoon fads, and he was pretty certain he was hardened to this business.

Which was why he had been so surprised by how engaging he found Ruby and her friends: a simple doll and her stuffed zoo-animal companions that come to life when their child owner is alone with them. There was no pretense to them. No smug knowingness, as in so many other kids' show characters. No winking to the adult viewers. He had been stunned to find himself (dare he say it?) emotionally drawn to them.

He was even more shocked at how easily he had secured the rights. Just a week after his first encounter, he had managed to get invited to tea with the author and illustrator of the *Ruby* books—a literarily gifted dowager—and her UK agent. They had both seemed almost bewildered by Ruby's growing appeal, given that the first book, *Baby Ruby and Me*, had been published nearly 15 years before.

A few short conversations later (including a second lunch with his daughter in tow), and Sheldon had the North American distribution rights in hand. The author had been very generous with the terms; she was just glad that her work would be exposed to a larger audience. After kissing Charlotte good-bye, she had left Sheldon with the farewell remark, "Take care of my baby."

When he got back to the States, his gut instinct about Ruby proved right. Hoping to shore up its preschool lineup, the top children's programming network had quickly licensed the UK version of the cartoon from him. Though it had needed significant reworking for a U.S. audience, it climbed to number three in the ratings in just six months and was now garnering a respectable 2.1 rating and a 16 share among kids aged two to 11.

Perhaps more important, Ruby appealed to diverse demographics. Older Americans were watching in droves, thanks to the nostalgic, carefree undertones and high-quality story lines of the program. Parents were finding it a perfect solution for cross-generational viewing in its time slot. This was the kind of news that advertisers, not to mention licensers, loved to hear. The iron was definitely hot, and it felt like the time to strike.

Swimming to the pool's edge, Sheldon checked his watch. He needed to hurry if he was going to make his appointment with the studio.

Masters of the Universe

Sheldon had been in countless offices designed to impress, but this one always succeeded. Thirty-five stories up a Century City tower and surrounded by glass, it made him feel like a goldfish in an airborne fishbowl.

The studio's proposed terms for a Baby Ruby feature film were lousy, even for a relatively untested property, and now Sheldon needed to negotiate a better deal.

"I don't know how you did it, but you got me!" Sam Fielding, vice president of licensing at Galaxy Pictures, blew into his own office like a whirlwind. The ritual backslapping and arm grabbing that followed was still a bit off-putting to Sheldon, even after 20 years in the business. Sam flopped into a large leather sofa by an incongruous fireplace and started in.

"This Ruby thing is going to be fantastic! We're really excited here. I can't tell you."

Sheldon allowed himself to relax just a little.

"But I can't lie to you either, Shel. We need this to be big. The summer is . . . well, the summer is leaving a little to be desired."

Sheldon knew that both of Galaxy's much-hyped summer films had been panned. Children's fare had been the wrong call, as families were unexpectedly leaning more toward action flicks.

"That's why I need you to muster the full strength of MMW's licensing capabilities behind this thing. I don't know how we managed to let you keep the promotional rights, Sheldon, but that's okay; we'll go with it. But I am going to need a licensing plan to support this deal that makes those King Lizard things look like niche marketing. I'm talking apparel, toys, stationery, meal promotions—the works. Don't even think of leaving anything out. I want to see Ruby collectible spoons.

"Baby Ruby has got to be everywhere this Christmas," Sam continued, "or I'll never get the numbers I need. And that would be bad all around. You know what I mean?"

Sheldon wondered whether this was a veiled threat aimed at MMW's other business dealings with Galaxy or merely harmless hyperbole.

"So you've got to show me what you can do with this thing before we close this deal. And I want to close this—soon. I know you're anxious to start working with us on picking the voices for Ruby and her friends. Who are you thinking of for Ruby?"

Before Sheldon could answer, Sam's assistant interrupted to remind him of his next meeting, for which he was already ten minutes late. Smiling as he escorted Sheldon to the door, Sam finished the conversation by saying, "We'll have plenty of time to discuss this out on the Vineyard. You'll be there, right? Great!" A moment later, Sheldon was on an elevator, sinking out of sight.

Sheldon had never even touched on the reason he had arranged the meeting in the first place.

Baby Steps

A week later, Sheldon met with Greg Caldor, MMW's top licensing director, to review the numbers on Ruby's performance at the international licensing show. Though it had fewer than 150 attendees when it began in the mid-1980s, the convention now attracted more than 10,000 visitors and 500 exhibitors—a testament to how important licensing had become for global business in just the past 20 years.

"There's good news and bad news," Greg started. "And worse news."

Sheldon had put Greg in charge of Baby Ruby's merchandise-licensing program while he had continued to work on the comprehensive plan. He trusted him as a friend as well as a colleague. "The good news is, our booth was swamped. Ruby was the belle of the ball. Everybody wanted her. They loved the giveaways, too."

Sheldon braced for what he knew would come next.

"The bad news is, the numbers are small. Times are hard. Everybody's hurting. *Planet Battles III* did less than a hundred million in retail this year. The ware-

---

The good news is, Ruby was the belle of the ball. The bad news is, the numbers are small.

---

houses are stuffed. Nobody wants to make big investments or commitments right now, especially in an untested property."

"But what about the show's rating numbers? And the book sales?" Sheldon asked.

"They like what they see so far; they just haven't seen enough. The show isn't even a year old. Who's to say what folks will think of it next year? You can't blame them for being cautious. Ruby's still the new kid on the block, so to speak."

Sheldon was getting ready to argue the point, but he changed his mind. "So what's the worse news?"

"They all want exclusives," Greg said with a grimace.

Sheldon knew this was coming. It was a growing trend in the business. He could negotiate around many of these requests, but he would have to give in to some. Exclusives lowered licensers' risk and improved their margins, but it meant that the total fee on the table for Ruby might actually be 25% less than he had originally projected, maybe even 50% less.

"And all the proposals came with long-term renewal options." That was the clincher. It ensured that if Sheldon did decide to make a big splash early with Ruby, he couldn't renegotiate better deals for a long time.

"I know you think this doll is more than just another pretty face, Sheldon, but if you wait till next year, who knows what you'll get? Heck," Greg continued, "put this off another two weeks, and I can't guarantee we'll still have what's on the table right now."

Greg was right. Interest in a property rarely comes around a second time. Licensers know they have a lot of choices, and they like to be treated that way—even when the property is red-hot. If Sheldon wanted to let the Baby Ruby property mature, he would have to play his cards very carefully.

"We haven't got long. Christmas is going to be decided in the next three weeks. After that, it's over."

Is a Ruby Forever?

Four days later, fresh from a business lunch at Santa Monica's L.A. Farm, Sheldon pointed his convertible toward Beverly Hills and MMW's Wilshire Boulevard office. Before he headed off to Martha's Vineyard on a two-week working vacation, Sheldon had an appointment to see his boss, Charles "Charlie" Masters, chairman and CEO of MMW. Sheldon considered himself lucky to be working for one of the fathers of the industry, and he was hoping for some good advice. For all his successful years in the business, Sheldon had never managed to acquire an evergreen property—one that threw off significant licensing fees for a long period of time. Charlie, on the other hand, had more than a dozen to his name.

Charlie had founded MMW after being entrusted early on with the syndication and licensing rights for the world's longest-running comic strip. He had built an entire company around his success with this one strip, but over the years, the firm had also acquired a wide portfolio of brands, including the very successful but short-lived ones Sheldon brought in. Charlie welcomed Sheldon into his office like a son.

"You know, Sheldon, I can't tell you what to do," Charlie began. "I built this firm by trusting the instincts of capable people like you. People who know how to do what's best for their clients and our firm without my interference." He slowly leaned back in his chair.

"But I will say this, I think you've got a real opportunity on your hands. It's just my opinion, but I like what I see in Ruby. It's basic. It gets to the core of what people are, and what they want to be. It could be a real treasure."

"So you think Ruby is my evergreen?" Sheldon asked. "I should move slowly on this one?"

Charlie paused long enough to let Sheldon recognize he had interrupted him. Then Charlie continued, "When I built up my classics, it was a different world. We sold cartoons door-to-door, city by city. When you went into a town, if you didn't sell it to the *Times*, you drove over and sold it to the *Daily News* or the *Tribune*. Today you can hardly even find a town with more than one newspaper.

"Back then, people weren't interested in wearing comic-book characters on their clothes, and especially not in the places they put them now. Cartoons were just animated comic strips, not a lifestyle choice."

He took a moment to think. "I guess what I'm saying is that there was less opportunity back then—but maybe more of it. Sure, there's more licensing now—$80 billion by the last figure I saw," he said, pointing to a dog-eared copy of a licensing newsletter. "But now even the good stuff has to contend with a thousand other 'maybe' properties.

"You have the sports-licensing trend, which is coming on the heels of the corporate brand-licensing trend. All of which hurts the character business—I don't have to tell you that."

Sensing that he was hardly relieving Sheldon's apprehension, Charlie shifted into managerial mode.

"But if you believe in a property, in your client, you have to do what's best for them, even if it means passing up the easy money today. Sure, the firm has been going through a rough patch lately—the declines in syndications are going to continue to hurt us for a while—but we'll survive. If you want to go slow on this one, tell the studios they can have her next year, and don't worry about what our partners will say. I'll handle that noisy gaggle of geese myself."

Baby or Bathwater?

Stepping into the Black Dog Tavern on Martha's Vineyard, Sheldon surveyed the crowd. As he expected, the bar area was overflowing; yet as luck would have it, Q&G's Bill Westman had managed to find Galaxy's Sam Fielding. They were engrossed in a lively discussion, but Sheldon couldn't tell whether they were talking boats or business. Spotting Sheldon, they waved him over. As he struggled through the crowd, he could make out only snippets of their conversation.

". . . she's got tremendous potential . . ."

". . . best in class . . ."

". . . she needs . . ."

". . . but is it too violent?"

Sheldon was busy trying to piece their conversation together, particularly the part about being too violent (surely they weren't talking about Baby Ruby?), when he heard a booming voice: "So Shelly, how about it?

Are we going to make something of this Ruby of yours, or what?"

Both heads turned to look directly at Sheldon, and the noise level in the bar seemed to drop. Sheldon searched for the right words in the relative silence. But which words should he use?

What's the Best Strategy for Baby Ruby?

Four commentators offer expert advice.

➤ Grant McCracken

Grant McCracken is a visiting scholar at McGill University in Montreal and the author of Culture and Consumption: New Approaches to the Symbolic Character of Consumer Goods and Activities *(Indiana University Press, 1991).*

Sheldon Bloomfield is operating in a pop culture market that is very different from the one that prevailed when his boss, Charlie Masters, started out in this business. The flow-through rate is much faster. In other words, many new properties make a big splash, grab their 15 minutes of fame, and then recede just as quickly into oblivion. Can Sheldon achieve longevity for Baby Ruby? Is there some way he can create a great sailing ship of a brand—something with deep, ballasted meanings that are stable and high-rigging ones that shift constantly in response to new trends? Sheldon senses he has a tall ship in the Baby Ruby property—and he could be right.

To find out, he needs to consult the gods of marketing. The place to start is with Theodore Levitt's fundamental question, "What business are you in?" (that is, What is the real opportunity here?). Then he should ask Robert Dolan's questions: "Where does value exist? How is it created? What's the best way of capturing it?"

There are several pieces to the Baby Ruby property: the books, the television show, the proposed movies, and the various merchandise licenses. The books created a platform for the TV show, the TV show creates a platform for the movies, and the movies create a platform for the licenses. In a perfect world, each platform creates value for the next one.

Sheldon, however, is not living in a perfect world. The Quick & Good Burger agreement feels to me like a value burn. In other words, it may well cost more value than it would create. Yes, it would be lucrative, but it also might push this sleepy little children's story from the top of the pop culture mountain straight down the luge run. There is nothing quite as tacky as fast-food plastic, and nothing quite as over as last week's fast-food promotion.

The problem, of course, is that the licensing deal is the price Sheldon must pay in order to get the three-picture deal he needs. Assuming good execution, three films would make an enormous contribution to the value of the brand and to its chance of achieving evergreen status. But the studio executives have made it absolutely clear: They want a licensing promotion out there beating the drum for Baby Ruby. They don't care about the long-term consequences of a licensing blitz—and they shouldn't. It's Sheldon's job to worry about that.

So Sheldon is caught. Licensing will help him get the movie deal, but it may well eat up much of the value the movie deal can create. This, then, is his first calculation: Will the licensing deal cost more value than the movies create? We are still not very good at running numbers like these (because, of course, these are not numbers but a complicated set of considerations that require a full and nuanced knowledge of the promotional and movie world). There's not much in the marketing playbook here; it remains more of a rough science than a fine art.

The second calculation is this: How little x can Sheldon give up and still get y? Sheldon needs to come up with a licensing package that increases his odds of signing the coveted three-picture deal without wounding his equity or compromising his chances of building an evergreen property. One way to accomplish this is to work with licensers to design promotions that both capture *and* create value.

This is a classic problem in marketing, and there are no easy answers. But when Ruby's creator said, "Take care of my baby," she certainly did not mean that Sheldon should turn it into a cheap fast-food toy or a collectible spoon. If Sheldon aspires to a career like Charlie's, he needs to let his evergreens grow for a while, before he starts trimming them with junk.

➤ Jack Soden

Jack Soden is the CEO of Elvis Presley Enterprises in Memphis, Tennessee.

Elvis Presley Enterprises is in a unique position: We don't usually knock on doors trying to make licensing agreements. Probably 95% of our partnerships are proposed by other companies. That doesn't mean we're not proactive. We put ourselves out there—for instance, we try to be a significant presence at the big New York licensing show—but we know we're lucky in that we're on a lot of people's radar.

The Elvis brand is now firmly established in our culture, but I have faced some of the same challenges Sheldon does here. When we were planning to open Graceland, Elvis had been dead four years. Record sales and various merchandising deals had spiked right after his death, but by 1981 they were all on the decline. We were opening Graceland mostly out of necessity: The estate's resources were dwindling, and there was a strong desire not to sell it or auction off its contents. We asked ourselves, "Should we put all our nets in the water and try to catch a lot of fish for one or two years and then retool for a quieter existence?" In the end, we relied on our optimism that the strength of the Elvis brand would last for years to come.

Sheldon has to decide how strongly he believes in Baby Ruby. All the signs point to her longevity, which is why he should hold out for better deals. After all, this guy has been in children's properties for a long time, but he still found himself emotionally drawn to Baby Ruby. That's a real connection that probably wouldn't have happened with the Teletubbies or Barney. The short but successful six-month run on television is another good sign, and the cross-generational audience is key. I can't help but think of Winnie-the-Pooh. Initially a character in a book, Pooh found a niche with young and old alike. I don't recall that there was ever a year that Pooh was the hottest thing in America or the world, but I'm sure you couldn't find anybody who wouldn't love to own that franchise. And like Pooh's sidekicks—Tigger, Eeyore, and the rest—Baby Ruby's animal friends each could be fleshed out over time.

Sheldon shouldn't be swayed by licensing director Greg Caldor. Greg thinks that if they don't act now, they might not have any deals in a couple of weeks. But if you really believe that you have to strike right this instant, then you're just throwing everything against the wall to see what sticks. That's no way to manage a brand. Besides, it's not like the market is red-hot. The movie deal offered to them was, in Sheldon's own words, "lousy."

My advice to Sheldon is to get on a plane to London, build on his relationship with the author, and secure the rights to the rest of the world. Otherwise, he could peddle hard in North America just to watch companies in other major markets reap the benefits. Then he should go back to Galaxy Pictures knowing exactly what terms he wants. If the folks there balk, he should walk away: The film deal might be much better in another year, when the TV show has gained more fans. Sheldon also needs to get involved with the *Baby Ruby* books, even if it's only from a communications standpoint. The better the books are positioned and marketed, the better it is for all his related financial interests.

Sheldon should also be careful about the types of products he licenses. At Elvis Presley Enterprises, many companies approach us with well-intentioned ideas that from our point of view would be, if not disastrous, a mistake. So we say no a lot, but at the same time we look for opportunities that will elevate and enhance the brand. For Baby Ruby, some products seem like a natural fit: plush toys, educational toys, collectible dolls, even apparel, if it's upscale. And because adults are watching the TV show with their kids, items like greeting cards, which parents usually select, would do well.

It seems to me that Baby Ruby is Sheldon's best shot at a long-term winner. He needs to trust his gut on this and make decisions that will build up the brand, not sell it out.

➤ Timothy Rothwell

Timothy Rothwell is a senior vice president of Universal Studios Consumer Products Group in Universal City, California.

As those of us who work in the field of entertainment licensing and merchandising know, Sheldon's in a tough spot. Even though he's got a promising property, he's competing for the same consumer dollars that corporate, sport, fashion, and art brands are vying for. Given the glut of choices out there, it's hard to be certain that Baby Ruby will make it big. But in my opinion, Sheldon's got to go for it. The U.S. licensing market is a $70 billion industry, so if Baby Ruby becomes a big hit, Sheldon will have struck gold.

I believe that, with this character, Sheldon has finally found his evergreen property. Sure, there are challenges, but Sheldon is in a very strong position to manage this brand upward successfully. And contrary to what the case study suggests, he doesn't have to choose between building an evergreen brand and signing licensing and promotional deals now. In fact, if Sheldon chooses the right partners, the deals he makes won't weaken the brand; instead, they'll help push Baby Ruby to the next level. As I see it, here's how Sheldon can build the property into a perennial revenue stream:

Publishing. Sheldon should find a strong North American publisher that will take on the distribution rights for the *Baby Ruby* books and build additional awareness of the brand. Many retailers and promotional partners will be eager to associate their names with the pure and innocent qualities of Baby Ruby. In fact, those traits remind me of Curious George, a property I've worked with that has enjoyed tremendous success across multiple platforms.

Television. All of the dominant character licenses in the marketplace today (SpongeBob SquarePants, Bob the Builder, and so on) are buoyed by TV. Retailers prefer to stock products based on TV shows (as opposed to movies) because their shelf life is usually longer; hence, they deliver a better return. Sheldon has the number three show in the country, so he's in good shape to begin a Baby Ruby merchandising and licensing program to complement the show.

Licensing. Because it typically takes anywhere from 12 to 18 months for products like toys and interactive games to go from contract to delivery, Sheldon would be wise to accelerate his licensing efforts right now. He shouldn't worry about the small numbers; he should focus instead on partnering with best-in-class manufacturers. If the licensing program captures the true essence of the Baby Ruby brand, the royalty checks will start rolling in—greatly exceeding any minimum guaranteed payments.

Promotions. The deal with Quick & Good Burger will add valuable exposure to the Baby Ruby brand. Again, Sheldon should stop worrying about the numbers being adjusted downward. Sealing this deal will put him in a significantly stronger position to secure new promotional partners that will be willing to spend media dollars in categories such as cereal, candy, snacks, and beverages. Creating a positive buzz in the marketplace will greatly enhance Baby Ruby's chances of success.

Film. The timing of Galaxy Pictures' movie proposal isn't right. I'd advise Sheldon to listen to CEO Charlie Masters and hold off for a while in order to let the property build momentum. If the Baby Ruby TV show continues to do well, and Sheldon can put together a successful merchandising and promotional program, the studio will be back with an even sweeter proposal. It doesn't make sense to contractually obligate your company to a "lousy" deal when your brand is just beginning to take off.

With the proper development strategy, Baby Ruby will continue to be a television hit—and that will spawn licensing and promotion deals that will take it to the next level.

➤ Bill Griffith

Bill Griffith's comic strip, Zippy the Pinhead, *appears in around 200 newspapers daily.*

I'm the creator of Zippy, a microcephalic, muumuu-wearing "wise fool." You might think that a property like that would be immune to mass-merchandising overtures—Zippy is no Baby Ruby. But I've seen my share of offers. A lot of corporations are interested in stuff that's on the edge because they've seen huge hits evolve from what were once cult phenomena.

The problem is that corporations don't want a character like Zippy for what it is; they want it for what they can change it into. Their aim is to retain some aspects but make the character more palatable to a wider audience. A perfect example came up in a meeting I once had with Disney, where the reps raised the question, "Can we lose the stubble?" (Zippy's chin always sports about a two-day growth.) I said, "Well, no. That's his look. But you must've noticed that he had the stubble, and that it's persistent—it doesn't come and go." I actually tried to make a case for stubble for about 15 minutes. But ultimately they explained their concern, that "Zippy might frighten small children." They were looking ahead to exploiting the property in amusement parks and thought a big, Zippy-headed greeter with stubble would be scary. All I could say was, "Yeah, it probably would." That meeting was over five or ten minutes later.

If you set out to create a property strictly as a commercial enterprise and have no real emotional attachment to it, a meeting like that won't bother you. But my intention with the *Zippy* strip never was for it to be something like *Dilbert*, which Scott Adams went after like a business venture—polling his readers and adjusting the strip to please the most people. I come from the opposite perspective; I do *Zippy* to express my thoughts, my opinions, my artistic vision. Whether a lot of other people want to read it is a secondary consideration. And as for the question, Do I want to change it so that even more people will read it? The answer is no.

So for me, the most disturbing part of this case was how easily the artist—who seems to have a real emotional attachment to her character—signed away all of her licensing rights. Unfortunately, it's very common for artists to do this. In my field, it's so difficult to get a daily comic strip syndicated that, when a syndicate does knock on their door, cartoonists pretty much will just roll over and say yes to everything. But they don't have to. For instance, when I first agreed to syndicate *Zippy* through King Features, I insisted that I keep the copyright, which at the time was unusual. I also stipulated that all prior merchandising deals remain in force as structured, and I retained all rights to nonprint media. A licensing partner can always come back later and ask for more, and you can renegotiate if you want. But if you give everything away at the beginning, it's all over.

Would Zippy, and I, be better off today if I had given up more control and struck more licensing deals? I did have somewhat of an illusion in, maybe, the late 1970s, when I first started getting movie offers, that—yes, Zippy is not for everybody and yes, Zippy is weird—maybe there's a bigger audience out there than I ever realized. Other weird things had broken through and become huge hits; maybe Zippy could be one of them. For a few years, maybe more than a few, maybe ten, I kind of believed that and pursued the offers.

But I think that the limited amount of merchandising I've done has worked for me, because it's kept Zippy in front of the right audience. It still has to be described as a cult audience, but it's a hard-core cult that keeps getting bigger, and it's endured for 30 years. I'm perfectly happy with that.

Originally published in December 2002

Reprint R0212A

ANAND P. RAMAN

The Global Brand Face-Off

Executive Summary

Espoir Cosmetics has received a tantalizing offer: sponsorship of the sequel to the Hollywood hit *Diana's She Devils*. For Natasha Singh, the U.S.-based company's global marketing officer, the movie is an ideal vehicle for global brand building. As the film is released in each country, Espoir can launch tie-in lipsticks and nail polishes.

But some of Espoir's regional executives don't see it that way. One of them—Vasylko Mazur, the head of Eastern European operations and Tasha's old friend—is particularly upset. The promotion will be expensive, and he doesn't like headquarters trying to control his strategy. "Tasha," he says, "you don't realize how different Eastern Europe is from the rest of the world. Movie-based promotions won't do anything for my sales."

Tasha understands his point of view. When she was Espoir's marketing head in India, she had to fight for her unconventional local initiatives. But she has come to believe that tastes are changing rapidly all over the world. From Eastern Europe to the smallest towns in India, customers want the products they see on TV, in the movies, and in international magazines.

Should Espoir take its new branding initiative global? Offering their perspectives on this fictional case study are Peter M. Thompson, the president and CEO of PepsiCo Beverages International; Jennifer L. Aaker, an associate professor of marketing at Stanford Business School; Harish Manwani and Simon Clift, executives of Unilever; and Masaaki Kotabe, a professor of international business at Temple University.

Natasha Singh was amused to see almost every guest at the black-tie gala sporting the same futuristic sunglasses. It was past 10 PM in Los Angeles, and the party to celebrate the release of the summer's most anticipated movie, *The Grid Revisited*, was heating up. Earlier that evening, a select audience had watched the long-awaited sequel to the 1998 blockbuster *The Grid*, and the scene-stealers had once again proved to be the lead pair's eyewear. In fact, there had been a near stampede when the invitees realized that each of the goody bags of *TGR* memorabilia contained a pair of the new shades, designed by the legendary Tom Strider.

Singh, the executive vice president and global marketing officer of one of the world's best-known cosmetics companies, $1.1 billion Espoir Cosmetics, rarely found the time to attend such events. When she wasn't visiting one of the 75-odd countries where the company marketed lipstick and nail polish, she liked to spend time with her husband and 12-year-old daughter. But her friends at Supreme Studios, which had produced the blockbuster, had insisted that she should attend, along with Espoir's chairman and CEO, Ed Johnson—and Tasha knew why.

Just as she had given up hope of spotting her boss in the melee, she heard his deep baritone behind her. "There you are. I knew I'd eventually find you," Johnson called out. As she turned to greet him, Singh was surprised to see Johnson triumphantly brandishing a pair of Strider shades. Noticing her expression, he chuckled. "My son, who's studying Spanish in Peru this summer, wanted them. You gotta hand it to this guy Strider, eh? He's got a global cult following for his product, thanks to some sci-fi movie," Johnson said as he looked around the crowded ballroom.

Singh couldn't have asked for a better cue. She grabbed two flutes of champagne, handed one to Johnson, and determinedly steered him to a deserted alcove. "Ed, I want to bounce an idea off you, and it can't wait. I started talking to some people at Supreme Studios six months ago, and they've offered Espoir the cosmetics sponsorship for the second *Diana's She Devils* movie."

"Is that why those folks were so keen to have me come here tonight?" asked Johnson, his eyebrows shooting into his hairline.

"They'd want you here anyway, I'm sure. But it's true they're looking for a decision. And I'd love to ink the deal soon," replied Singh enthusiastically. "*Diana's She Devils* was a hit two years ago, and our research suggests that the sequel will probably be an even bigger draw. There are more romantic elements in it, by the way. Most important, I've seen the studio's publicity plans. They're huge. And we can associate Espoir's new summer line with the release all over the world."

"We've been offered deals like this in the past," Johnson pointed out. "But we never thought it was worth the money. And particularly if it's only our summer products range—"

"Here's why I think it's right for us now," Singh cut in. "First, we should be doing something splashy—next year is our 50th anniversary, after all. Second, this is an ideal vehicle to launch a global brand-building strategy. Think about it, Ed. The three stars are from Europe, Asia, and South America—our fastest-growing markets. And they're all on board for the sequel. What if we created three new lipstick and nail polish combinations, in the right palette for each of the three stars, and then associated the stars with the advertising? As the film gets released in each country, we can launch the new products in specially designed combination packs."

"And call it Espoir's anniversary line," Johnson chimed in. "Interesting. But where does the money for the promotion and the related advertising come from? I don't think you have enough in your budget."

"I don't," replied Singh, her nose wrinkling slightly. "But I know where to find it. I had lunch last week with Brian Davis." She was referring to the marketing head for North America. "He loved the idea. As he sees it, two of the stars also happen to represent big ethnic markets in the U.S., so he's more than willing to foot some of the bill. Now I just need to get the other regions to chip in, which shouldn't be so hard."

Johnson frowned. "I wouldn't be too sure about that," he said slowly. "If the recession in the U.S. gets any worse, and it may, I'll have to cut marketing budgets again. In that case, the country heads will have little left for local advertising or promotion initiatives after paying for your global promotion. They aren't going to like that very much, and they'll blame you if they don't meet targets. If I were you, I'd check with the regions before going any further."

"Well, I'm off next week to Europe and South Asia, so I'll sound them out in person," said Singh, a trifle defensively.

"Good," said Johnson, ushering Singh back into the thick of the party. "Let's talk when you get back."

Je Reviens

As the airplane rose into the bright blue sky over Paris, Singh's spirits soared with it. She pulled out a laptop to write up her notes on her discussions with Jacques Dubois, Espoir's newly appointed marketing head for Europe. Belying her apprehension, the young Frenchman had warmed to the idea of a big movie-based promotion to mark the company's golden anniversary. He admitted that Espoir's archrival, Revlon, had boosted top-of-mind awareness by tying in with movies like the 2002 Bond film, *Die Another Day*, and he was ready to fight fire with fire.

A flash of European pride had, however, showed itself when Singh mentioned her wish to set up a central Web site that would allow people to buy customized products from Espoir. She wanted to test the initiative first in North America and extend it to Europe once the logistics were in place. "That will not work. A Web site for European customers must have a different look and feel from the American site. It should also have a different name if it is to appeal to them," Dubois had immediately declared.

Although Singh had agreed to think about it, she wondered if the possibility that he could be wrong ever crossed Dubois's mind. Now, reflecting on that moment of irritation, she couldn't help but smirk; that must have been how she had seemed to her own colleagues back in 1994. After all, she'd been more than a little self-confident when she took over as the company's marketing head in India. Espoir, which sold a wide range of cosmetics and accessories, was the leading mass-market brand in North America and Western Europe. Despite the global cachet and the pent-up demand for foreign cosmetics, however, the company had been unable to make any headway in the competitive South Asian market.

When Singh was being interviewed for the job in Delhi, she had been quick to point out why. "I can get a facial for Rs 300 [$6.66] and a manicure for Rs 75 in a beauty parlor. Why would I pay Rs 120 for a lipstick or Rs 75 for a nail polish?" she demanded. Although the comment annoyed the multinational's top brass, they gave her the job. Those had been heady days, recalled Singh, who had cut her marketing teeth at two British multinationals in India after graduating from the prestigious Indian Institute of Management at Ahmedabad. She had slashed product prices, reduced pack sizes, and used, for Espoir, unusual retailing tactics. For instance, since there were no chains like CVS and Walgreen's in India, Espoir had been selling its products only at the handful of department stores in the four largest metropolitan areas. So Singh reduced prices and sizes and made sure Espoir items were available in all the hole-in-the-wall grocery stores in the cities and, later, even many of the towns. Espoir couldn't use large counters in those stores, so trays of lipsticks and nail polishes were placed invitingly near the cashiers. That was a tactic Espoir's top brass hadn't even considered. In five short years, the company became one of the market leaders in the Indian market.

Johnson was so impressed by Singh's performance that after three more years he offered her the newly created position of global marketing officer. By that time, Espoir's sales were growing faster in Western Europe, Asia, and South Asia than in North America. "We need to develop a more cohesive brand identity by coordinating local strategies and find a way of leveraging synergies across markets," Johnson said at the time of her promotion, about a year ago now. "You're in an ideal position to do that, because people respect you—but they also know you'll be sensitive to local issues. The job might not win you any popularity contests, but I know you'll get it done."

The announcement that the aircraft was beginning its descent into Kiev's Boryspil Airport interrupted Singh's reverie. As she leaned forward to look down at the Dnieper River, she wondered how her old colleague in arms, Vasylko Mazur, the head of Espoir's operations in Eastern Europe, was faring. They had first met five years ago at a leadership training program in Los Angeles and had spent some long evenings sampling California wines and griping about top management attitudes toward developing markets. They had stayed in touch until recently. Singh realized that Mazur had dropped out of sight after taking over as the head of Espoir's Eastern European operations six months ago. It would be good to talk to him again, she thought as she fastened her seat belt.

An Ugly Wrinkle

Kiev was glowing green and gold at the end of a perfect summer day. The gilded tower atop St. Sophie's Cathedral cast burnished shadows on Mykhailiwska Square, a short distance from Espoir's offices. But neither Singh nor Mazur noticed. They had been at each other's throats from the moment she broached the idea of a global promotion.

"Vasylko, you are being entirely unreasonable," said an exasperated Singh.

"Me? Or you?" retorted Mazur, puffing furiously at the cigarette that never seemed to leave his lips. "Tasha, you don't realize how different Eastern Europe is from the rest of the world. Movie-based promotions won't do anything for my sales. We are in the beauty business, not the movie business." He tried again to convince Singh that appointing beauty queens like Miss Russia and Miss Ukraine as brand ambassadors would strike a chord with customers in Eastern Europe. Not only would it be cost-effective, it would also allow Mazur to create a contest-based promotion. "Customers will write in with suggestions for new colors, each beauty queen will pick her favorite, and there will be lots and lots of prizes. You, of all people, should know what I'm talking about," he said pointedly.

Singh winced. Her rows with Espoir's headquarters were part of company folklore. She had insisted on launching nail polish in eight-milliliter bottles (price: Rs 35) in India rather than the standard 12-milliliter bottles (price: Rs 75). That would encourage customers to sample, she argued, and allow Espoir to take on the local market leader, which sold a 12-milliliter bottle for Rs 30. "You do know that we have sold our products in only one size all over the world," she had been told initially. The next year, Singh had insisted that Espoir create a range of products in purple because that had been the rage in traditional Indian dresses like the sari and the lehnga that year. The palette was alien to Espoir, which usually stuck to beiges and reds, but it did wonders for the brand in India.

"Vasylko, you are being unfair. First, I did all that ten years ago," argued Singh. "It was a different world then, and India was different, too. Second, I've stayed away from beauty contests because they are off brand. The Espoir woman is smart, independent, a risk taker. She doesn't identify with pageant queens. Third, I've chosen colors for the global promotion that will work in Eastern Europe. If you won't believe me, test-market them yourself, and I'll be receptive to any changes you can show me we need."

"You should hear yourself talk," scoffed Mazur. "Do you remember how we used to mock HQ, saying how little it knew of our countries? You now sound like an HQ person, who can only see the logic of creating a global brand, using a global campaign, and sticking to a global positioning. Very little of that works here! You must let me handle the market the way I think best. Did a global strategy work for you in India? If it didn't, how can you try to sell me one now?"

"Because a global strategy can work, in India and in Eastern Europe, too," Singh shot back. "Do you remember Operation Second Coat, which I spoke about at our annual conference three years ago? We had to launch global colors in India because our customers started asking why they weren't available. We used those products to segment the market and shifted

---

"Your global promotion smacks of a narrow vision, and there is no scope to adapt it for this market. Moreover, the promotion will eat into my marketing budget, and I cannot afford that."

---

many customers from a less expensive local line to a more expensive international range. By the time I left, we were increasingly using global ad campaigns. I'll admit we modified them sometimes, but they were essentially—"

"That's not what you used to say," Mazur interrupted, grinding his cigarette into an overflowing ashtray. "In any case, I want no part of your global promotion. It smacks of a narrow vision, and there is no scope to adapt it for this market. Moreover, the promotion will eat into my marketing budget, and I cannot afford that. I need to be quick, tactical, and responsive to local needs, and your templates and rules about standardization only slow me down. I will worry about being in sync with the global brand after Espoir has become the market leader in Eastern Europe."

Cosmetic Differences

The weekend at her parents' farmhouse on the outskirts of Delhi was a welcome break for Singh. Family gossip relegated the tensions of Kiev to the back of her mind and helped her recover a little from jet lag.

As she walked briskly into the glass-and-concrete tower that housed Espoir's India office in the city of Gurgaon, near Delhi, on Monday morning, Singh literally bumped into Ravi Narayan, who had taken over from her as the head of South Asia marketing. "Good job on the signage at the airport, Ravi," she said enthusiastically. "I saw the new backlit signs at JFK and Charles De Gaulle, and it's great to see them at Indira Gandhi International too. How are we doing?"

"Not badly," Narayan replied as he escorted her to the 20th-floor conference room that served as Singh's office when she was visiting. "Our market share rose by two points last quarter. However, the market isn't growing as fast as I thought it would. In addition, competition is getting stiffer since several Asian brands have launched their products in India in the last six months. Local brands are offering large discounts, and direct marketing in cosmetics is catching on. It's a cruel market."

"Is that putting pressure on prices?" Singh asked immediately.

"No," replied Narayan. "We've managed to hold prices until now. In fact, our premium line is doing quite well in the metropolises. Many more department stores have opened in the last 12 months, and that has eased the retailing bottlenecks."

"I was amazed to see two more department stores in this area since my last trip," agreed Singh. "I went to one over the weekend and felt I was already back in L.A. Almost every big American brand seems to be available here now."

Narayan laughed. "That's nothing, Tasha," he said. "You should see how things are changing beyond the big cities. A couple of months ago, I went on a market reconnaissance trip to Chandigarh and decided to drive the 260 kilometers there. I couldn't believe my eyes. All along the way, I saw farmers using cell phones, there was an Internet café every two miles, and rooftops were crowded with satellite television dishes. Almost every town I drove through had billboards for *Cosmo, Elle*—or *Friends*!"

"What does that mean for us?" asked Singh, all ears now.

"I suspect consumer habits are changing faster than we imagine," replied Narayan. "I stopped at a gas station in the small town of Shahabad and checked out a nearby grocery store. The shop counter was full of trays containing cosmetics, and I counted at least three local brands and two global brands, including Espoir. Two teenagers were looking for a nail polish but couldn't find what they wanted. They kept asking for the latest color that they had seen advertised on an English serial the previous evening. The shopkeeper had to promise to order it for them before they would go away. What struck me later was that not once did the girls ask how much the latest nail polish would cost."

"I guess the cost-benefit equation in towns works closer to the way it operates in cities today," suggested Singh. "All our customers want to be, for want of a better phrase, with it. Earlier, the point of reference

---

"A global strategy will resonate in India in some cases, but I doubt if we will be able to do away with local marketing initiatives. It's tough to overcome cultural differences."

---

used to be the nearest big city; it's the world now. Don't forget that the 100-odd satellite television channels we receive in Delhi are available in small towns, too. The Internet allows people to access information about the rest of the world from anywhere. People are traveling abroad much more than they used to. That's why I've believed for some time that we can afford to be more global in our approach to markets like India."

Narayan shot Singh a wary glance. "That's tricky. A global strategy will resonate in India in some cases, but I doubt if we will be able to do away with local marketing initiatives. There are large income differences in India, and it all depends on the market you want to tap. Moreover, it's tough to overcome cultural differences. You've lived in the U.S. for over a year, but that's tea you're drinking—not coffee. In any case, what do you have in mind?"

Hope Springs Eternal

Three days later, Singh walked into Johnson's penthouse office suite in Espoir Tower in downtown Los Angeles. She handed him a box of the champagne-filled truffles from Paris that he loved.

"That means trouble," groaned Johnson in mock despair. "By the way, the Supreme Studios people have been hounding me in your absence." He popped a chocolate into his mouth and commanded: "Talk."

"I've had mixed reactions to the global promotion. Dubois was supportive, Mazur hated it, and Narayan was willing to give it a shot," Singh reported.

"Really?" Johnson asked. "I thought India would be the least interested in a Hollywood film-based promo. Aren't Bollywood films more popular there?"

Singh snorted. "Last year, Bollywood had just one hit while Hollywood had six hits at the Indian box office. *Spider-Man, Harry Potter, Lord of the Rings*, et cetera, et cetera, et cetera—they all made more money in India than Bollywood productions."

"Interesting," said Johnson. "What's changed?"

"For one thing, the international studios have improved the dubbing of English movies in local languages," Singh explained. "And import regulations have eased, so films can be released in India a lot faster, sometimes within days of the U.S. release. Basically, people like good films regardless of where they're made. So tying in with the *Diana's She Devils* project makes sense for India—and most of our other markets, too."

"But not everyone agrees?" asked Johnson.

"No," sighed Singh. "And of course I see why. Every country head believes his or her country is unique. And it's risky for them to pin their hopes on a global promotion when they've never done so before. But what's the point of doing business in a global marketplace if we don't leverage the opportunities that globalization presents?"

"Let me play devil's advocate for a moment. Most companies I've seen try global game plans have failed at them," cautioned Johnson. "The global tactics tend to either overstandardize or oversimplify, and they discourage local innovation. What's more, I'm not sure our brand has the same image all over the world. Why should we waste money on a global campaign that may end up confusing our customers?"

"We will save costs by building brands through global strategies and allowing local initiatives to drive sales," Singh pointed out. "Most managers concede that the quality of campaigns we produce is better than those done locally."

"I need to see some research to prove that a worldwide initiative will save Espoir money. Barring a handful of exceptions, I have yet to see global projects generate economies of scale," Johnson said. "There are also organizational issues. Who will take responsibility for the success of the anniversary line after its launch? You? Or the regional heads, who follow your dictates without conviction? The promotion won't be a success if it proceeds on autopilot."

"Those issues can be worked out. In fact, I've been meaning to talk to you about the kind of global-brand team we need to have," said Singh. "But we should go ahead with the movie tie-in. At best, it will reinforce the brand's equity. At worst, we will learn some lessons about where global promotions don't work. Since the initiative will boost sales in North America at least, what do we have to lose?"

"Vasylko Mazur, for one," said Johnson somberly. "After your visit to Kiev, he wrote to me. He's pretty upset at the prospect of our trying to control his marketing strategy."

"Are you saying he's threatened to put in his papers?" asked Singh, startled.

"It was more than implied. But look, I only mention it because it raises the larger issue. How hard should we be pushing a global strategy?"

Should Espoir Take Its New Branding Initiative Global?

Five commentators offer expert advice.

➤ Peter M. Thompson

Peter M. Thompson is the president and CEO of PepsiCo Beverages International, based in Purchase, New York.

Natasha Singh is on the right track, but she faces a twofold challenge. She has to keep Espoir's marketing programs and strategies relevant to local markets even as she leverages global scale and best practices. And she has to get the buy-in of frontline executives because that's critical for the successful execution of global initiatives.

Singh correctly sees the consumer and retailer needs for achieving some global consistency, and the sponsorship she is pushing could be an effective global program. But to succeed, she has to rethink her role. Singh has to become less of a developer and more of an orchestrator. My experience at PepsiCo leads to four recommendations.

- Headquarters should involve local teams in shaping the global marketing agenda. At PepsiCo Beverages International, the chief marketing officer leads a worldwide network of managers, who meet at least three times a year. The executives share best practices and choose ideas that the global team or a region should implement. The network develops the sense that it owns the programs, so there is peer pressure on managers to use them. By sharing responsibility, Singh could source global ideas from her network rather than trying to impose HQ's ideas. Local PepsiCo managers signed up the Spice Girls (before they became international stars), Ricky Martin, and Shakira as brand ambassadors, and we leveraged them around the world.

- Espoir should develop a shared vision of its global brand-building model. Singh should identify the non-negotiable areas where global consistency will be the rule: name and look, positioning, a base of global colors, and quality standards. Other areas, such as price and pack strategy, selection of local colors, and channel strategy, should be the responsibility of managers in the field. For instance, in the case of Lay's, we established a universal "gold standard" with common specifications for base potato chips to maximize global consistency and economies of scale. However, we recognized the need for flexibility to address local tastes with different seasonings and even to allow use of acquired strong local brands instead of the Lay's name.

- Singh should create a menu that allows local choices. She could maximize the buy-in for her ideas by developing global promotion platforms that leave room for country variations. PepsiCo Beverages International may create a team of internationally known soccer stars, for instance, and suggest how the team can be used by local managers. A country team can boost the program by hiring a local star. Singh could easily take that route in Eastern Europe: A local event using one of the Hollywood stars along with Miss Ukraine could be a great promotion.

- She should quantify both the benefits and costs of global consistency. Singh should make it possible for Vasylko Mazur to base his decision on a cost-benefit analysis. She should provide a comparison of the cost of executing her program in the Ukraine with the cost of the local promotion. Mazur would then see how much additional media weight could be put behind the campaign because of the global program's savings on production and other costs. That additional media muscle would be a compelling argument in favor of adoption. At PepsiCo, we drive home the cost-benefit trade-off by charging country managers for the use of our global advertising pool and sponsorships. So when local managers buy into a global event, they have an incentive to see that it gets executed well.

Espoir cannot reinvent the wheel for every market it enters. However, achieving both global scale and local relevance requires time and a flexible approach. Singh should have started the alignment process earlier. If it is too late to get Mazur on board, she must defer to the local team's judgment. Mazur knows the retailers and the local competition, and he is on the hook for the numbers. The energy he will put into the local initiative will generate more sales for Espoir than a halfhearted buy-in to Singh's global program.

➤ Jennifer L. Aaker

Jennifer L. Aaker is an associate professor of marketing and the A. Michael Spence Scholar at the Graduate School of Business at Stanford University in California.

At Espoir, as at many multinationals, there is a tension between the need to create a global brand and the desire to retain a focus on the local customer. How should companies manage that tension, in terms of both strategy and execution?

First, successful global marketing companies make sure that their definition of a global brand, and their vision of global brand building, is widely understood within the organization. That is important because no two managers instinctively think of the concept the same way. It is unclear what Singh means by a global brand and whether her field managers would define it differently. If they do not develop a common understanding, Singh and the local managers will not work effectively as a team to build a global brand.

Singh must also realize that for most companies, global brands are not manufactured or marketed the same way in every country (the definition of the global corporation as selling the same things in the same way everywhere was provocatively put forth by Theodore Levitt in an HBR article, "The Globalization of Markets," May–June 1983). At most firms, the definition is looser than that: A global brand is a brand that is available in many nations, and though it may differ from country to country, the versions have a common goal and a similar identity. That definition gives local managers a great deal of freedom to make decisions on building and managing the brand—decisions that often decide its overall success or failure.

Second, most companies distinguish between strategy and execution when trying to build global brands. For instance, Intel has created an Intel Voice, which is used to develop marketing communications. It highlights five global goals (build Intel equity, achieve consistent results, save time and money, connect with audiences, and do your best work) and a common brand personality (intelligent, innovative leader). The corporate headquarters has also provided guidelines for visual style (clarity, simplicity, and originality). While Intel managers everywhere try to attain the same goals, they retain considerable control over the execution of campaigns. Such flexibility would go a long way toward getting local managers such as Mazur and Dubois to buy into Singh's ideas.

Third, smart companies have instituted formal structures, processes, and measurement systems to build global brands. At Espoir, the CEO has created the position of global marketing officer, but he hasn't put in place a structure to help Singh do her job. For instance, P&G empowers country teams to develop breakthrough brand-building programs. Will Singh work with such teams? Nestlé, by contrast, has a global unit that encourages the adoption of best practices and programs across markets. Is that the template the CEO has in mind?

It is equally important for Espoir to create a measurement system that will evaluate whether global marketing efforts and local efforts are meeting goals. With such a system, Singh could use data to show why her global campaign would work in Eastern Europe. If she could not make a convincing case, she would have to let Mazur launch his local promotion, but she could push him to measure the success of his strategy against the company's goals. Only measurement will allow the debate over localization versus standardization to take place at a more sophisticated level the next time Singh comes calling on Mazur.

Finally, the companies I've studied have understood every nuance of their target markets and global brands. For example, Singh wants a global focus on the "smart, independent" woman. But a smart, independent woman in the

United States may differ from one in Eastern Europe. How does Singh know that participation in beauty contests is inconsistent with being smart and independent in the Ukraine? She must accept that the manner in which a global brand talks to its audience will often vary in different parts of the world.

➤ Harish Manwani and Simon Clift

Harish Manwani and Simon Clift are executives of Unilever. Manwani is president, Home and Personal Care: Latin America; Clift is president, Marketing: Home and Personal Care.

Companies have to harness the coherence and scale of a global brand as well as the closeness to the customer of a local brand if they wish to succeed in today's competitive marketplace. It makes sound business sense, therefore, for multinational companies like Espoir to manage some elements of the marketing locally, some regionally, and some globally.

Many brands are capable of generating universal appeal, as Singh has noticed. That is certainly true of brands whose international nature is intrinsic to their equity, such as fragrances and prestige products, but it is also true of brands like Espoir. In a more open and connected world, brand equity has to be managed more coherently than it used to be in terms of positioning, communication, packaging, and even pricing. However, this does not necessarily mean that the absolute price should be the same in every country; the price should be relative to what the market can bear. Creating a more uniform brand identity forces managers to make trade-offs between the benefits of addressing markets through a coherent brand and the advantages of adapting it to address each market differently. The trick is striking the right balance between being mindlessly global and hopelessly local.

Companies have to organize themselves to develop innovations regionally and globally, not just locally. In most industries, the quality of innovations and the speed with which they are developed have become critical for success. A vibrant brand requires a regular stream of exciting new features and continuous updating. But the costs of innovation are so high that it makes financial sense only in the largest markets or, preferably, when resources can be pooled regionally or globally. In fact, because of the scarcity of development skills, such pooling of resources is necessary in order for companies to compete effectively.

Singh is correct that to manage the equity of a brand globally, it is important that the advertising idea be consistent across markets. However, she should not force the same execution in all markets. If celebrity endorsements are central to the advertising idea, the selection of the celebrity or the situation can vary according to the local culture. Singh's aim should be to communicate effectively and not seek sameness if it does not add value to the brand. At the same time, we must point out that the starting point for managers like Vasylko Mazur should be why they cannot be similar rather than why they have to be different. That is often not the case.

Within a strategic brand framework, a critical element of success is the choice of how to "activate" the brand—how to deliver its message to consumers. This is best decided locally; for instance, country managers should be free to decide the kind of media and the nature of the promotions they want to use for an advertising campaign. Similarly, they must stick to standard packaging designs, but the materials they use could depend on local availability and cost structures. The choice of retail channels should also be left largely to local managers. However, with retail chains like Wal-Mart and Tesco becoming global operations, companies may have to lay down guidelines for international customers, too.

Striking the right balance between global strategy and local execution requires teamwork on the part of local managers and managers with global responsibility. For that kind of complementary interdependence to work, the company must have the right structure. So perhaps the most important aspects of managing a global brand are creating an appropriate organization, ensuring that roles are clear, and assigning accountability for each element of the marketing mix. The companies that manage this sort of teamwork best are those where values like sharing and interdependence are deeply embedded in the organization and internal communication systems are good. These companies direct their competitiveness toward the outside world and away from internal power struggles and turf wars—unlike Espoir.

➤ Masaaki "Mike" Kotabe

Masaaki "Mike" Kotabe is the Washburn Professor of International Business and Marketing and the director of research at the Institute of Global Management Studies of Temple University in Philadelphia. He is the author of a dozen books, including Global Marketing Management *with Kristiaan Helsen (Wiley, 2001) and* Market Revolution in Latin America: Beyond Mexico *with Ricardo Leal (Pergamon Press, 2001).*

The needs of consumers may be converging due to the Internet, satellite television, and international travel, but that does not mean consumers in every market will adopt the same products or brands. Singh forgets that globalization frees consumers from conformity and allows them to choose products from all over the world. As a result, people have become more selective than they used to be, and it has become extremely difficult for executives to pinpoint consumer preferences in many markets.

That, my experience shows, has two major implications for global marketers. First, one-size-fits-all global strategies may not be effective, even in countries where they used to work well. For example, the Guatemala-based fast-food chain Pollo Campero has been growing rapidly in the United States because consumers have an appetite for fried chicken that tastes different from KFC's. To retain its position as the market leader, KFC might have to cater to ethnic or regional tastes, too, instead of sticking to a strategy of homogeneity in its home market.

Second, the corporate headquarters cannot tackle the global-local dilemma on its own; it needs the help of local executives. Singh should develop a corporate-level marketing policy in consultation with senior executives from the company's key markets. She would face stiff resistance from the subsidiaries if she tried to impose her ideas on them, especially since they have been demanding more flexibility. However, both Singh and the country managers may be surprised to find that a policy will result in more, rather than less, standardization.

Espoir has to identify a core line of products that is standard across all markets, and it has to create lines that are country specific. That product mix will create the global image Singh desires and allow the variations that country managers want. It is not as impossible as it sounds. For instance, the Japanese version of the Honda Accord is small and sporty, the American model is relatively large, and the European edition is short and narrow, with the stiff and sporty ride Europeans prefer. Despite selling three kinds of Accords, Honda maintains a uniform image by emphasizing environmental friendliness and high performance in all three markets.

Espoir must use consistent marketing communications in order to reinforce its premium image. Instead of drawing up ad campaigns, Singh should draw up guidelines on the execution of advertising by local affiliates. For instance, Mercedes-Benz has a handbook that subsidiaries and sales agents must strictly follow while developing local advertising.

Sooner or later, Singh will also need to discuss pricing structures with local managers. Although the latter are charging premium prices for Espoir's products, those prices are relative to what local markets can bear. Large price differences between countries spawn gray-market actions by distributors, who ship products from low-price to high-price markets. To curb that, Singh will have to narrow cross-border price disparities, but she cannot do so without the support of local executives.

I suspect that the company's retailing strategy needs to be coordinated across countries, too. My research shows that a two-pronged strategy works in the case of premium products like cosmetics because there are both upscale and aspiring consumers in every market. Since Singh learned to shift aspiring customers from lower-end to higher-end products in India, she should encourage local executives to do the same thing.

Thus, there is nothing wrong with Singh's global strategy, but the manner in which she is trying to implement it is incorrect. She has forgotten the time it took to turn around Espoir in India, and success has made her overconfident. Singh would do well to remember that no empire was built in a day.

Originally published in June 2003

Reprint R0306A

DAWN IACOBUCCI

The Quality Improvement Customers Didn't Want

Executive Summary

Is investing in new technology always the right choice for a company and its customers?

Allan Moulter, the CEO of Quality Care, isn't sure he wants to invest in the computerized reception system that consultant Jack Zadow has outlined for him. But in this HBR case study, the argument Zadow makes is impossible to ignore. Quality Care's rivals have invested in similar systems or are planning to do so. The new system promises to take care of routine busywork, freeing staff up for other interactions with patients. It seems as if the competition hasn't even cut staff and is counting on increased customer retention to pay for the investment.

And yet, Quality Care's surveys of its own customers show that they prefer the human touch when checking in. How would customers feel if the first "person" they met when they came in the door turned out to be a machine? Moulter prides himself on his responsiveness to customers. And with 86% of Quality Care's customers either satisfied or completely satisfied, aren't things fine as they are?

Has Moulter considered all the facets of his predicament? How will Quality Care's staff be affected by a decision one way or another? What about the costs of upgrading the system? Can Quality Care maintain its standing without going high-tech? Would customers rebel when confronted with the proposed reception area or would they appreciate the increased efficiency? Six experts weigh the costs and benefits of technology in a service industry.

Jack Zadow, the consultant, was persuasive. Wrapping up the hourlong presentation, he still seemed as energized as he had in the first five minutes. "Your biggest competitor, HealthCare One, has already begun using a computerized reception system in 14 of its 22 facilities," he said, pointing to the overhead projection illuminating the darkened conference room. The image was a regional map with red stars on every HealthCare One facility and yellow circles around the ones using the new system. "When their members come in the door, they go right to a computer and slide their identification card through. Then the computer leads them through a set of questions about their current medical condition, the reason for the visit, and so on. Everything is done electronically: The computer pulls the member's record, processes the new information, and then routes the member to the appropriate staff person for consultation."

He slipped the next image over the map. It showed Quality Care's own facilities in dull brown. "HealthCare One will have all its facilities up and running on the new system by June. The number two player, Medi-Centers, is planning to install a similar system by January 1997. I think you should consider it seriously—it's really the wave of the future."

The last overhead. A model of a "new and improved" Quality Care reception area. No more crowded waiting room. Patients talking with nurses in the privacy of small, partitioned cubicles. Other patients checking in, paying bills, even having their blood pressure taken at attractive computer stations.

"I think this one speaks for itself." Jack let the image sink in for a moment. "But I'll comment anyway. With this system, you take a giant step forward in the quality of your service. Your staff will be able to devote more energy to making sure that each patient receives prompt, unhurried, personal attention." He switched off the projector and stepped back to flip on the lights.

Blinking, Allan Moulter accepted the report summary Jack handed him. He had been the CEO at Quality Care for nine years—how many meetings did that mean he had attended? He looked at Pat Penstone, the company's CIO. She seemed enraptured. He rubbed his forehead. "Thanks, that was informative," he said. "You've given us a good overview of an intriguing trend in service delivery in the industry—at a regional level and at a national level. But can you tell us a little more about the specifics of installing a system like that? How is HealthCare One handling the transition?

How has it measured the improvements in service quality? How much has the company invested in training? Computer consultants? Troubleshooters? Health-Care One is a staff-model HMO like us, so I know we can look at them for comparison, but I have to say that I'm a little concerned. You seem to be telling us that our image as a quality health care provider will suffer if we don't make this move, but we're talking about an important change in a lot of daily routines. We have just under 3,000 employees and 200,000 members. Think of the procedural changes. The timing changes. And with more automation, wouldn't we want to think about cutting the administrative staff by what, by two at each facility? Four? Six?"

"You could cut several positions from each location," Jack said. "But HealthCare One isn't cutting staff—this is strictly a quality improvement, and it's paying for itself in increased customer retention over the long term. What's more, the transition isn't difficult. In the pilot location, they're already testing the next generation of the system. Artificial intelligence diagnostic programs. They're incorporating scales and the blood pressure machines you saw in the last overhead. That saves a step or two for the nurse practitioner, so it simplifies service operations. They're also going to upgrade so that the computer will be able to produce records that can be standardized for insurance companies. Within a few months, the nurses and physicians will be experimenting with a prototype for their own notes on patients, which will streamline follow-up care as well."

"If they're not cutting staff, and they're investing in new generations of the system, where's the real advantage? There is a cost-control element to consider as well, isn't there?" Allan looked around the room, then back at Jack. "The system itself is a big investment—it would run the company more than $350,000 when you include development, installation, training, consulting, and so forth. What's more, the network would have to operate across all of our locations. And if we wanted to do it right, we would probably tackle a whole host of ancillary projects at the same time, things like rethinking the design of our reception areas and our workstations.

"I'm not sure it's worth it. Our customer retention rates are good. They've been steady for the past two years. And our customers are satisfied with the service—on a scale of one to five, 86% of our customers are either a four—that's satisfied—or a five—that's completely satisfied. We survey them constantly.

"Frankly, I'm not convinced that investing in a new system will improve the quality of our care. As I said, you're talking about a major shift in how our people get their work done—all the way up the line. That's disruptive. Would the gains be worth it?"

"Ultimately," Jack said patiently, "if your staff is less stressed and your care is more personalized, your quality improves. And—this is almost more important, although it's going to sound strange—the *image* of your quality also improves. Remember, the top two

---

"I'd hate to see the rest of the industry moving towards this technology while we do nothing."

HMOs in this region are installing this system. Quality Care is the number three player—you can't afford to look as though you're behind the times."

Pat could not contain herself.

"I'd hate to see the industry moving toward this technology while we sit on our hands doing nothing," she said, straight to Allan. "I mean, okay, it's just the reception function, but what if a patient assumes that because we're not high tech with our sign-in procedures, we're also not up to speed on our medical procedures? The reception area, taken alone, isn't a big deal. But as a part of our whole offering, it's critical. It's the first thing our customers see. It tells them what we are and how we work."

She nodded at Jack and continued. "Not to mention that we'll have to install a system like this at some point anyway, as soon as the government or the insurance companies decide that it's the way to go. Once a method is standardized, we don't want to be playing catch-up."

"Right. Well." Allan looked at his watch, an impassive expression on his face. "I can see this warrants some further discussion, but we'll have to leave it for the time being." He stood up, ending the meeting. "Jack, thanks," he said again. "We'll go over the reports and I'll see you later this week."

Back in his office, Allan swallowed two aspirin with the one gulp of coffee he had left in his mug. Then he reached for the box of crackers he kept in his top drawer. He knew he should get some lunch, but he wanted to think about this issue some more without distraction. The afternoon was booked solid; then he wanted to catch at least part of his son's ice hockey game at 5:30, and he had to be back in town to participate in a panel discussion on health care for the elderly at 8:00. Munching, he thought about Quality Care's position in the market and the kinds of things that had made the company successful to date.

Quality Care had never been the region's largest or most profitable HMO. But it was doing well. This past year, its total revenues were $450 million, with profits of $8.1 million after expenses. And it did have a good track record when it came to customer retention. Businesses kept the contract because their employees were satisfied with Quality Care, and Allan liked to think that he had played an important role in creating that loyalty.

Allan had begun his career with a large manufacturer of electronics equipment, where talking with customers had been his passion. He had brought that passion to Quality Care. During his tenure, the HMO had instituted regular customer satisfaction surveys. Patients were asked how they felt about the service they received: Were they waiting too long to see a doctor? Were they satisfied with the location and upkeep of the facilities? Did they want more information on health clubs or wellness programs? One survey had revealed the need for increased communication with pregnant members. Now expectant mothers received regular

---

Quality Care frequently surveyed its corporate members, affiliated hospitals and health clubs, even its own employees.

---

newsletters geared to provide timely advice and support during their pregnancies. The company had also provided a dedicated toll-free number so that pregnant customers would have easy access to advice and information. Allan was proud of the program.

And the surveys weren't the only way the company solicited information from its customers. Each facility also had a "feedback box" in the waiting area—paper and pens were provided, and patients were encouraged to offer anonymous comments on any aspect of their experience with the company. In addition, Quality Care frequently and systematically surveyed other constituents: its corporate members, affiliated hospitals and health clubs, even its own employees.

His peers often complained about how hard it was to increase customer satisfaction these days. Allan knew why it was so hard—keeping all the constituents happy was an insane balancing act. Still, Allan figured it was the open communication and the feedback that kept the company effective and competitive.

That's why he was more than a little concerned about Jack's presentation. Quality Care's own marketing staff hadn't turned up any dissatisfaction with the current reception procedures. And yet Allan was drawn to the possibilities presented by the new system. He picked up his phone and punched in Ginger Rooney's extension. Ginger was the vice president of marketing for Quality Care. She was part of the team that was scoping out locations for expansion and possible new alliances. She had flown in from Pittsburgh that morning—too late to attend Jack's presentation.

"Do you have a minute right now to hear about that meeting?" Allan asked. She was in his office moments later, folder in hand.

"Cracker?" he offered, holding out the box. She declined. He took another one and plunged into the topic.

"I'm not entirely convinced we need this system," Allan said. "But I'll tell you, I was playing devil's advocate in there, and I was having a hard time. I don't want us to fall behind the curve."

"We're ahead of the curve, if anything," said Ginger, holding a familiar survey report out for his inspection. "Why you and Pat are so gung ho about this computerized reception area, I'll never know. If you'll remember, we were approached by a sales rep from the Technomedic Software Company 18 months ago. We looked into a similar system then and dismissed the idea. We took the concept to our members in a special survey and they said they'd hate it."

"But then why would HealthCare One go forward with it? They're the one to beat. I know they must have

---

"We spent a lot of time and money on that special study—why are you so willing to disregard it?"

---

done their homework on this—maybe better than we did. Don't take this the wrong way, but they've got a more sophisticated organization. I'm sure they've weighed the risks against the benefits. Our study might have been inaccurate. Is it possible that the results are out of date already?"

Ginger didn't take offense. "I doubt it," she said mildly. "Think about why the customers said they wouldn't like it. Human contact versus machine. Health care is a personal field—one-on-one attention is what makes a satisfied customer. They just didn't like the idea of a computer, at least for this part of their interaction with the HMO. They come into one of our facilities for some health-related exam. Often it's just routine, but sometimes they're a little nervous and they appreciate all the human contact they can get. It's reassuring. The idea of having the first 'person' they meet when they come in the door turn out to be a machine was quite disconcerting to many of the people we surveyed. Especially the seniors." She fell silent, but spoke again as she saw Allan framing a response. "We spent a lot of time and money on that special study—why are you so willing to disregard it?"

"Look at ATMs," Allan said. "Older people got used to them."

"I'm not sure that's true. And even so, does that mean that we'll try to encourage all our members to use the computer but that we'll need human receptionists anyway for older members? Isn't that making the operation more complicated, not less? That doesn't sound like cost savings or quality improvement to me."

"We've invested a good deal in Zadow's research as well," Allan said. "HealthCare One hasn't reduced staff, but we could. And what happens when all the other organizations have signed on and the government or the insurance companies start requiring standardized reports? Pat brought that up in the meeting. It's a valid concern."

"There's more than one way to create a standard report." Ginger began to look frustrated. "I'll bet half the time, the patients enter information incorrectly anyway. Someone would have to double-check the files on a daily basis."

She returned to his earlier point. "If HealthCare One hasn't cut staff, how can you be sure that we would be able to? And keep in mind who we should really be talking about—the customers. Their perception is what's important. Remember, our *employees* were the only ones who really liked the idea. The administrative staff thought that a computerized reception area would make their jobs easier. And the nurse practitioners have so many routine procedures to do that they're just racing patients by on a conveyor belt. They thought the system would give them time for the human touch."

"Now you sound like you're arguing for the system, Ginger. You can't disregard employee input. Our employee turnover rate is average for this industry, but it has increased over the last two years. That's a reason to reconsider the system in light of Jack's report," Allan said. "It's important to keep our employees happy—we want to keep good people. In fact, as I recall, it took a lot of tap dancing to explain to them why we weren't proceeding with the computer system last time."

"But the point still remains that the members didn't like the idea," Ginger said. "They thought that it was just another sign of big corporate America depersonalizing something that in this case happens to be one of the most personal services there is. You mentioned us retaining our 'leading edge' image. But a computer sends an impersonal image as well. I just don't think that a computer at the front desk will make or break us. You know that my department's reports consistently show favorable customer satisfaction results. They already think we're doing a good job by them. If I can be blunt, I think that you've been romanced by a consultant's very savvy presentation. And I think that we've spent so much money on the consultant that you feel we wouldn't get our money's worth if we didn't follow his recommendations. I seem to be the only one thinking about what's right for the company."

"Ginger, what happens in a year or so when everyone but us has this system installed?" Allan threw up his hands. "Don't you find it strange that we're trying to choose between installing a system that we think might enhance our quality as a provider and not installing a system because we want to please our members?"

Ginger spotted Pat in line at the cafeteria on the first floor of the building that housed Quality Care's administrative offices. She caught up with her just as Pat was paying for lunch. "Not to ruin your digestion, but I have a problem I'd like to talk about with you for a few minutes. Do you mind?"

"Not at all." Pat smiled. Ginger knew the smile was strained. The two had just never really gotten along. For people whose departments were usually in agreement about new initiatives and plans for the company, Pat and Ginger had often found themselves holding opposing views, or at least misunderstanding each other's motives.

"I'll get right to the point, and I won't take much of your time. I know that you support the idea of a computerized reception area, but I'd like to know more about why. You know that the customers are not in favor of it."

"No, I don't really know that." Pat looked uncomfortable for a moment and then seemed to gain resolve. "I may as well say this. I know that Allan has a personal interest in how the company communicates with customers, but I have some serious doubts about the way all of those customer satisfaction surveys are carried out. You don't personally oversee the surveys, do you? That's Mike Farrow's bailiwick, isn't it?"

"Yes, it is," Ginger said. "But we use the same sorts of surveys as most companies do. Frankly, I do agree with you about some of that. I don't put much stake in some of the information we get from the complaint boxes, for example. Those comments reflect the views of only one person. 'Change the night you're open late from Monday to Thursday.' 'Change the color scheme in the examining rooms.' Those comments aren't significant. But we asked a significant number of our

---

"You say you're thinking of the bottom line, but which one?" she asked. "Today's or tomorrow's?"

---

members straight out, in a special study, how they would feel about a computerized system. They said they wouldn't like it."

"I just don't have a sense that any of that information is to be trusted. People need to be told what they want—and people will recognize quality care when they see it. That's why I think we need this system."

"I'm thinking about the bottom line," Ginger said. She wished she had waited until later in the afternoon to approach Pat. In fact, she wished she had written her a memo and sent it over by e-mail. "Why go through all the trauma if we already know how the customers will receive the change?"

Pat hadn't yet touched her lunch. She picked up a packet of salad dressing and pulled it open. "You say you're thinking of the bottom line, but which one?" she asked. "Today's or tomorrow's?"

Should Quality Care Install the New System?

Six experts examine the effect of new technology on customer satisfaction.

➤ Thomas O. Jones

Thomas O. Jones is president of Elm Square Technologies, a company based in Andover, Massachusetts, that is developing advanced customer-service software.

This is a no-brainer: Quality Care should develop and install the new reception system. It will increase value to the customer as well as overall customer satisfaction, improve employee morale, and provide a strong financial return with a relatively small risk.

When customers are asked for feedback on a proposed change that is hard to picture, managers should not put too much stake in their responses. Listening to customers is critical, but in certain situations a company must rely on other methods to determine whether customers will value a proposed change. The input that Quality Care has received from its customers seems to indicate that putting in a computerized reception system would be a poor use of resources. However, there are several reasons to conclude just the opposite.

First, customers traditionally find it extremely difficult to envision the benefits of technology, particularly when it replaces an interaction with a live person. In a survey conducted for a company in an industry related to health care, 82% of the customers said that they would not like the proposed automated customer interface. But when managers went ahead with the installation, 71% of the customers immediately chose to use it. And in subsequent dealings with the company, every customer who tried the system continued to use it.

Second, when customers are given a choice between speed and accuracy on the one hand, and comfort and caring on the other, all customers are not the same. In the population at large, most customers will opt first for speed and accuracy and then for comfort and caring. Interactions with caring, live people can have a profoundly positive effect on a service experience, but not as a replacement for prompt and proficient basic service. There will always be those who choose human interaction over convenience, notably customers experiencing serious illnesses and older patients who have trouble with newer technologies or unfamiliar environments. Overall, however, a computerized reception system will provide a more streamlined, more reliable, less stressful, and in many ways more enjoyable experience for the incoming customer.

Third, when it comes to customer satisfaction, Quality Care is not doing as well as it might seem. Allan Moulter says that 86% of the company's customers are either a four or a five on the five-point scale. He seems pleased with that. Yet research has demonstrated that only fives are truly loyal. This means that a significant percentage of the company's customers are not completely satisfied; their accounts are at risk. Quite apart from reaching a decision on the new system, Quality Care must direct some attention toward staying competitive on its base product offering. If it does not, all the additional services it contemplates will have little effect.

Fourth, the change will provide the employees with the benefits of new infrastructure, an increase in their own capability, and, without heavy cuts in staff, the ability to focus on other activities more valued by the customer. What's more, in terms of service management, the system will provide brutally accurate information about service delivery levels—including actual waiting times. Better measurement of the customer's experience can lead to significant improvements.

Finally, what appears to be a major investment really isn't—or at least shouldn't be. The reception function represents the rest of what Quality Care does; commitment to new technology here shows a commitment to new technology in general. Even if the project eventually were to cost over a million dollars, the capital expense for such an investment over five years would be roughly $300,000 per year. If the staff were reduced by only five or six people across the entire organization, the savings would offset that expense.

How should Quality Care move ahead? Assuming for a moment that there is no opportunity to create a prototype for testing, the company should at least create a mock-up version for use in focus-group testing. The user interface should be designed with great care—it should be extremely friendly, even to the point of using a full-motion video "attendant" to lead the customer through the process. Moulter should make sure that every element of the design is customer tested.

Then, after carefully designing the processes and training the employees, Quality Care should install the system in a single location. The company must ensure a comfortable, non-frenetic environment during the initial test. Customers should be given a choice between unattended use of the system, attended use of the system, and interaction with a live receptionist. The system should be portrayed as a service enhancement—not as a further dehumanization of the health care system.

If experience in the financial services, food services, and hospitality industries provides any indication, a very large portion of the customer base will view the system as increased value, and the company can certainly support those who don't. This case shows the myopic approach that many companies take to listening to customers. Customers are good at saying how they feel—but not how they would act in a situation they have never experienced.

➢ Mary Jo Bitner

Mary Jo Bitner is an associate professor of marketing and research director of the First Interstate Center for Services Marketing at Arizona State University in Tempe, Arizona. She is the coauthor of Services Marketing *(McGraw-Hill, 1996).*

Moulter's caution is well warranted. An automated reception system represents a major investment (in both dollar and people costs) with an uncertain payoff. And although the market leaders have decided to make the move, Moulter should not jump to install the new reception system out of fear that Quality Care will be left behind—especially in light of the results of Quality Care's customer research and the fact that customer satisfaction is not a particular problem for his company. That said, neither should he totally dismiss the idea. Investments aimed at improving quality should reflect customers' needs, but customers don't always know what they're going to want in the future, especially when technology is involved.

Instead, Moulter should put more time into analyzing the pros and cons of adopting this significant new service innovation. Research results consistently suggest that companies that spend time up front—testing and developing a concept, analyzing the financials, testing the market, and planning an implementation strategy—have the most success in introducing major new services. But those results are for companies who do *their own* research; Quality Care should not assume that HealthCare One has done its homework in this area. In fact, as part of Quality Care's research, Moulter may want to determine how the customers of HealthCare One and Medicenters are responding to the new systems.

Why go through all that? Why not just make a decision now? Because once a program of this size has been started, it is very difficult to reverse, even if levels of customer satisfaction drop and the new system does nothing to make the company more efficient. The cost of change will be great; the cost of backpedaling would be even greater—both in dollars and in further inconvenience for employees and customers as the company tried to regain lost ground and find a suitable course of action.

It is well known that for many services, a customer's first encounter with an organization can be the most critical. Moulter needs to think about how an automated reception encounter would affect his customers, who may be arriving for their appointments sick, unsure of themselves, and emotionally vulnerable. Would Quality Care retain its aura of intimacy and personal concern in an automated environment? In addition, Moulter should be aware that a computerized system would place new demands on customers, forcing them to become, essentially, part-time employees of the company. The customers would be providing part of their heath care service for themselves—and they may not want to do that.

Moulter must ask himself if it should be *employees'* perceptions of quality service that dictate how the system is designed and implemented. It would be far better to start with *customers'* perceptions and needs and then to work back into the system to determine the operating standards. Would the new system really meet customers' needs? The answer isn't clear.

There are two primary reasons to consider this investment: Either it should represent considerable cost savings (without sacrificing customer-defined quality), or it should significantly improve levels of customer satisfaction and retention. The big payoff for installing this particular system is stated as "increased customer retention over the long term." But since no one has had this type of system for very long, how was the potential benefit of long-term retention determined? Has Moulter truly calculated the costs and expected benefits in terms of retention? Has he pushed the consultant to determine the return on quality? Have the decision makers in this case factored in the costs of educating their customers, training their employees, and implementing the system? And have they considered the return on this investment versus the return on other changes Quality Care might make to enhance its image as a premier HMO? Moulter seems quite taken by the proposed system, but if there are no problems with the current reception process, perhaps other improvements should be made first.

Finally, Moulter must reconsider the idea that the new system will enhance Quality Care's image as a modern health care provider; that without it, the company will appear to be out of date. That may be true. But Rooney's concerns are equally valid. What about the possibility that customers may perceive Quality Care as cold, impersonal, and bureaucratic if the system is installed? There is more than one way to create a modern image; technology isn't always the answer.

➤ Eric Hanselman

*Eric Hanselman is a corporate systems engineering manager
at Bay Networks, based in Billerica, Massachusetts.*

Quality Care is grappling with a problem faced by many service-based businesses: How can a company adapt technology to help manage the flow of information while still presenting a personal face to the customer? It's never an easy task.

Right now, Moulter, Rooney, and Penstone seem to be focused on the wrong issues. The very idea of the new system has dazzled them; they've seen how their competitors are handling the technology; and they're proceeding as though this is an all-or-nothing decision. It isn't.

Unfortunately, too many managers in similar situations make the same mistake: They look at a working system and try to accommodate it rather than objectively assessing their own requirements. Moulter, Rooney, and Penstone need to examine their own goals and their customers' desires and *then* begin to plan a system for Quality Care. The company seems to have a unique strength in its rapport with customers. Its managers need to think about how that strength can be leveraged to help both the company and the customer.

First, they should consider the benefits and disadvantages of such a system for Quality Care's internal operations. It's clear that an automated system could take some of the drudgery out of the receptionists' jobs. But does

Moulter really know if the current process is problematic? Has that process contributed to Quality Care's increasing employee turnover? Moulter should apply the same tools he uses to measure customer satisfaction to internal issues. He should also give careful consideration to a point Rooney made: If the customers enter data, who is going to check the information that is entered? That sort of potential for error must be addressed early on.

Then they need to reevaluate the image factor. They seem to be concerned that the company will appear outdated if it doesn't install the new system. The automated reception service would certainly have enough IT glitz to make any technophiles among the customers or employees drool. But how valid is the concern about appearances? So far, the customer surveys have not revealed a desire for a high-tech image. And Penstone's attempt to invalidate the survey data has an unfortunate "I know best" ring to it.

It seems reasonable to assume that Moulter, Rooney, and Penstone will decide to proceed with some type of automated system. At that point, they must turn to the specifics of implementation. How can Quality Care take advantage of the value that the technology can add without losing the customer satisfaction levels that the current system generates? Rooney expressed concern about having two ways to handle customers, but realistically, a gradual change is the best option. By gradually phasing in the new system, both the employees and the customers will have time to get used to it, and the company will be in a better position to work out any problems along the way.

Quality Care might want to begin the transition by issuing customers a member identification card when they visit the office. (It sounds as though the company does not yet have such a system in place.) At first, the customers will not even need to know how to use the cards; Quality Care can begin by training the receptionists on a pilot system, and the patients can observe the receptionists "reading" the cards and using them to update patients' records.

Quality Care's IT group will be able to test the system, using the reception staff as trained operators in real time. It takes a good deal of effort to change the way a company deals with information; the more time the company has to observe and refine the process before rolling it out across the board, the better. In this case, a final system for customers' use would, most likely, be composed of a series of choices for answers to common questions. Having the reception staff act as intermediaries—asking customers the questions that will later be asked by the system—will let the company more accurately review the appropriateness of the questions. This is also an opportunity for Moulter to continue to pursue his passion for surveying opinions. Both customers and staff need to be polled about the system as it is developed.

Such an approach will also keep the initial costs down. At first, Quality Care's capital outlay will go only toward inexpensive card readers. The company can buy computer systems that are tough enough for customers to use when the system is more fully defined. The risks will be lowered as well. The reception staff will be able to revert to the old system in the event of any problems. The staff can also handle any anomalies that might arise.

To make the system work, it is important to offer clear value to the customer. At the outset, all customers should be presumed not to have a card. But as customers begin to return with cards, the company should set up priority reception desks at which those who have begun to use the system will be able to proceed more quickly to see the staff. As more and more of the customers are issued cards, more of the reception facilities should be dedicated to card processing. As long as members see that they get better service with the cards, they will be motivated to use them.

As more customers are issued cards, Quality Care can take the next step—inviting patients to check in by themselves. If surveys show that customers are comfortable using the cards, the company might also want to allow them to enter the reason for their visit and to check to see that their address and insurance information is correct. If an address needs to be changed, customers who checked in with their card should be given priority over customers who have not. Putting the card users back in line with other customers removes the benefit of using the cards and thus jeopardizes perceptions of their value.

Because the customer base is uneasy about technology, Moulter might want to consider a few options that would make the system less imposing. Pen and tablet computer systems, for example, are used like a clipboard. Checking off boxes on a form is much more friendly than punching keys at a computer station. And wireless technology would allow customers to register while sitting anywhere in the waiting room.

Although it is clear that Quality Care must move toward technology for solid business reasons, pursuing that path in a way that serves their customers will ensure that both today's and tomorrow's bottom line are healthy. Technological arguments should never override customer input. Technology should always be a tool—a means, not an end.

➤ Christopher A. Swan

Christopher A. Swan is the manager of British Airways' Marketplace Performance Unit, which is responsible for tracking the quality of the airline's performance from the customers' perspective.

This case highlights a common pitfall of the technology race: When one company adopts a new high-tech system, its competitors are often tempted to follow suit without enough research and reasoning. But a change that is right for one company may be wrong for another—even another in the same industry. Before Moulter invests in an automated reception system, he should figure out why Quality Care really needs it and what it can truly do for the company and its customers.

Despite the tone of the case, I suspect that HealthCare One and Medicenters have *not* introduced their new automated reception systems solely to benefit their customers. It is more likely that their motivation came from a different source.

For example, perhaps HealthCare One's back-office operations needed an overhaul. The case doesn't go into such detail, but billing and client records may be a disaster area for the market leader. The company may well be turning to high tech out of desperation.

Medicenters, on the other hand, may be using the technology as part of a strategy to protect itself from losing market share. Its system may have been installed with the primary purpose of monitoring customers so that the company can better understand and meet their needs. Its managers know that in order to retain market share, Medicenters must grow as fast as the market grows. They also know that if Quality Care's market share grows, it will be at the expense of competitors like Medicenters. The new system could be a defensive measure.

Either way, for HealthCare One and for Medicenters the "improved quality, customer benefits" positioning was probably an add-on. And either way, it doesn't matter. What matters is that each company probably did make sure that its new system's advantages would outweigh any disruption to the customers. Moulter needs to do the same.

It seems that Quality Care's back-office operations are in decent shape. If that is the case, then the company has time to experiment with the new technology's capabilities. Quality Care has the benefit of being able to observe two examples—and an opportunity to use technology to create real value by starting from its own customers and then working back through the organization.

First, the company will need to conduct more research. Moulter's current studies are tainted. Those customer surveys were completed before the new technology was in use anywhere in the market; once technology has been introduced, consumers' views can change rapidly. Moulter also needs to be sure that his new surveys probe customers' feelings on a whole host of topics; they should not be confined to questions about the existing uses of the new technology. The feedback may not appear to be technology oriented, but technology may prove to be the answer.

Then, based on the feedback, Quality Care can begin to respond. Essentially, Moulter will be using data on quality to build a business plan—and a technology plan. For example, one new survey might ask customers how long they're willing to wait on the phone for an answer to a question. If 76% of customers say that they are willing to wait for 10 minutes but are usually kept waiting for 20, then Moulter knows where there is an opportunity to improve service.

Once he does address the problem, he must be sure to close the loop and let customers know how the company has responded to their feedback. Perhaps Quality Care could include the information in a newsletter for customers: "Our computer systems now allow us to track your care—and your satisfaction with our service—more effectively. Here's what you're saying and here's what we're doing—through technology—to address your concerns. Six months ago, 76% of you let us know that you would be willing to wait up to ten minutes for an answer to a telephone query. We've since introduced a telephone monitoring system. Today 68% of our customers report that our response time has been cut to ten minutes. If you find that your experience with Quality Care's phone service has improved, we're delighted. If it has not, we want to know. Please call Rosie Smith in our customer service office at 222-1111, extension 123. We'll be sure to update you as we continue to improve."

In considering what technology can do for his customers, Moulter should ask what kinds of benefits they would perceive as valuable. Thinking again about the possibilities opened up by an automated reception system, perhaps Moulter could find out if patients would like to receive a monthly statement of their accounts. Or he could ask if they would value updates from their health records, including information on recent treatments and future appointments. The customers might say that they would find such information a reassuring indication that the company knows them personally and keeps track of their particular situations. If Moulter finds that such updates would be perceived as valuable, Quality Care could introduce them by saying: "Here's what technology can do for you. By using this new membership card, you'll help us generate complete and accurate reports on your health care, which will be sent to you on a monthly basis."

Putting in technology for its own sake—or solely for the sake of the company—misses the point. In Europe, airport concourses are littered with automatic ticket machines that you rarely see being used. These machines represent state-of-the-art technology that links into various airlines' central reservations systems and departure-control systems. They offer an extremely cost-effective way to sell tickets and check passengers in for flights. So why do customers avoid them, preferring instead to see a representative at a check-in desk? Because the customers see no personal benefit in using the technology. What's more, if a customer wants to have a particular seat and is unable to get it, or wants to make sure that a special meal or some other service requirement has been attended to, he or she has to go to the airline's customer service desk anyway.

Moulter has long understood that listening to customers and responding directly to their needs is a big part of what makes a company successful. He shouldn't abandon that practice now. By all means, Quality Care should avail itself of any back-office efficiencies that it can, but the company should not be pushed into cutting back on customer care—or looking as if it is doing so—simply because competitors are doing so for reasons of their own. Quality Care should adopt the technological improvements only if research shows that customers will come along because they want to, not because they have to.

➤ Teresa A. Swartz

Teresa A. Swartz is a professor of marketing and the marketing area coordinator at California Polytechnic State University in San Luis Obispo, California.

When Moulter joined Quality Care nine years ago, he brought with him a passion for customer service. In part, that passion is responsible for the company's current success. Quality Care has a track record of monitoring customer feedback and responding to it, as exhibited by the recent additions of the newsletter for pregnant members and the toll-free hotline offering advice and information. Current retention rates are strong, and customers seem satisfied—they stay with Quality Care by choice, not because they feel trapped. So why, at this critical juncture, would Moulter even consider disregarding his customers' input? Where has his passion gone? Moulter needs to be careful not to lose sight of his customers. Now is not the time to stop listening.

To help him decide whether to install the new reception system, Moulter should first consider the real motivation behind the idea. If quality improvement lies behind the investment, Moulter should determine the project's potential return on quality. Quality Care's customers don't have a problem with the current reception process, and past research indicates that they prefer "high touch" over high tech. There is little reason to believe that the return will be there for this particular investment.

There is, however, ample indication that improved information technology will become the new standard for the industry. Quality Care does not want to be left behind. Perhaps that is the true motivation behind this idea. If that is the case, fine; but then Moulter must approach the project from a different angle. This is not an all-or-nothing dilemma. Quality Care does not have to follow the competition blindly in determining what the new standards will entail.

Indeed, because Moulter has input from both internal customers (employees) and external customers (patients), he is in a wonderful position to forge a win-win solution to his problem. Although apparently at odds, both sets of customers can be satisfied.

Moulter should then think about what sorts of service the reception area currently offers. Whatever happens, Quality Care must somehow make sure that the start of the service encounter continues to take patients' emotions into account. Meeting that need—reducing patient anxiety—is critical if Quality Care is to maintain its satisfaction levels and retention rates. Armed with that understanding, Moulter can then more thoughtfully consider what his employees want. The nurse practitioners believe they could provide more human contact and personalized service if some of their duties, such as blood pressure readings and weigh-ins, were automated. In addition, the administrative staff members believe that a new system would make their jobs easier. Quality Care *is* its employees. Without a doubt, the company must support its staff if it wants to maintain or improve customer satisfaction and reduce employee turnover.

The solution? Quality Care should institute an advanced computerized system that its frontline employees can use *with* the patients. When patients arrive, staff members can greet them and assist them with processing the registration information. This will allow for the important human touch at the beginning of the service encounter. The high-tech aspect will still be present—much of the processing will be computerized—but, at least initially, the process will not be self-service. As a result, the new system will speed the flow but still allow for personal contact. Some aspects of the processing, such as blood pressure tests and weigh-ins, can be more fully automated from the initial launch, freeing up nurse practitioners for more contact with customers at more important stages. And over time, as customers become familiar with the computerized reception system, the company can encourage them to take advantage of the self-service options and staffing can be reduced. The total high-tech reception service can be offered, with "high touch" still available for those who prefer to be processed by Quality Care staff and for those who encounter problems during their self-service.

While this hybrid system would require a significant investment, the returns should be readily evident through increased customer satisfaction and retention as well as through increased efficiency and effectiveness. The system will provide all the benefits Moulter hopes for—improved patient records, immediate access to records, standardized reports, and higher-quality customer contact—but with much less risk. Contrary to what Penstone thinks, people do not need to be told what they want. The voice of the customer needs to be heard.

➤ Terri Capatosto

Terri Capatosto is an assistant vice president of communications at McDonald's Corporation, based in Oak Brook, Illinois. She oversees the customer satisfaction and media relations departments.

The top-level managers at Quality Care have spent a good deal of money investigating the merits of a new automated reception system and the possible reactions of customers, but they need to do more research to determine if installing such a system would be a good strategic move for their business. Overall, they don't yet have a solid understanding of the system's potential effect on profitability and efficiency. Therefore, I would recommend that they invest just a little more money on a trial test before making a choice one way or another.

First, Moulter should select a test location and resurvey the customers there, making sure that the survey questions clearly isolate the reception function from the rest of the health care experience. Right now, it seems that Quality Care's customers have been confronted with the whole range of possibilities ("it will check you in, *and* it will take your blood pressure, *and* it will weigh you, *and* it will schedule your next appointment"). What's more, the survey questions are probably too broad. The customers are confused, and that confusion is generating vague survey results.

Next, Moulter should install a model of the system at the test location. A "live test" will provide him with new information on several fronts. First, he'll find out whether his customers behave as they have said they would in previous surveys. Second, he can measure whether an automated reception process will affect usage—that is, whether customers will choose Quality Care over another provider. Third, he'll spot potential problems—such as inaccurate data entry—that can be more easily addressed early on.

Has anyone thought of how such a system would handle illiterate customers? Or language barriers? Or people with poor vision or dexterity?

Throughout the test, Moulter should keep his customers informed and continue to solicit their input. They should know why he is surveying them, what their feedback has indicated, and how the company intends to use the information. The more informed customers are, the more they'll feel that the company wants them to be involved in issues that affect them, and the happier they will be with whatever decision the company finally makes. Health care is a sensitive and highly personal service industry. If Moulter decides to go with the new system, his customers should understand why and exactly how they will benefit from it. If he decides against automation, that in itself could be a unique, positive point of differentiation for the company.

At McDonald's, we went through a similar decision-making process when we were looking into offering an 800 number to field customer inquiries, comments, compliments, and complaints. It was a big-ticket item, and there were a lot of considerations. If you are a customer-driven company, you have to listen to your customers. But you also have to strike a balance between what the customers are asking for and what you can do from a cost and benefit standpoint. We had to find out not only how our customers felt about an 800 number, but also if it affected their perception of McDonald's, their number of visits, and their level of satisfaction. So we conducted a test and surveyed our customers throughout the process. We kept track of their feelings about their experience with the 800 number and tried to determine if the number helped us recover and retain previously dissatisfied customers.

As for employee reaction to the proposed changes, Moulter needs to reassess some of the internal factors he thinks he has pinned down. For example, he knows that his employees believe that a new system would allow them to spend more quality time with patients. But what exactly will be going on during those minutes that he will save by installing a new reception system? Is there something currently lacking in the delivery of care, something that employees could provide if they had more time with each patient? When Moulter surveyed employees, did he simply ask them if they would like their jobs better if they didn't have to take patients' blood pressure? People always want their jobs to be easier—but unless Moulter asks pointed questions that isolate the factors he is trying to assess, he won't get the information he truly needs to measure. He needs to determine which actions take up the majority of each person's time at work and what impact the automated system would have on how and when various tasks get done.

Similarly, Moulter should rethink the customer studies he has already conducted. His current research seems incomplete. Has he looked at his results demographically? Do women tend to like the idea of a new system more than men? If, for example, women make up 90% of Quality Care's customer base, that information is going to be important. If senior citizens have an aversion to an automated reception area and seniors make up 60% of the company's customer base, then their feedback is going to be much more significant than if they make up only 20% of the customer base.

Moulter should also make more of an effort to understand his competitors' actions. His consultant has mentioned that HealthCare One is already upgrading its system. That fact seems to be putting pressure on Quality Care to catch up—but instead, it should be ringing an alarm bell. Moulter has considered the installation and training costs of a new system, but has he considered how quickly that system might become obsolete? How much reinvestment would be needed to keep it up-to-date and to keep employees and customers trained?

Finally, there's the issue of standardized reports for the government and for insurance agencies. This is pure conjecture in the case—but it does raise an interesting point. Would a system that speeds up interactions with insurers improve customers' satisfaction levels and benefit the bottom line? Are there other benefits or problems for the customer in that area? That, too, is worth studying. Moulter should start by contacting the relevant insurance agencies and government offices to find out if they have any plans to require a new reporting system, and if so, when it might go into effect. At this point, Moulter can only speculate about possible requirements; by the time they are in place— assuming they do materialize—the system Quality Care is looking at could be obsolete.

Currently, McDonald's is testing an initiative that would restructure the drive-through process. We're considering a face-to-face ordering system that would replace the intercom method of taking orders. Based on early projections, we suspect that such a change will result in faster, more accurate, and more personal service, and that customers will be more satisfied. But we're testing our assumptions rigorously.

It's tempting to read into preliminary survey results, but a gut feeling isn't enough—especially when considering a significant capital and developmental investment that would change a fundamental part of Quality Care's customer experience. Moulter needs to deal with clear, clean facts.

Originally published in January–February 1996

Reprint 96106

Keeping to the Fairway

Executive Summary

Sandy Michaels, chief marketing officer of financial services giant Pace Sterling, faces a tough dilemma now that the high-profile golf tournament her company sponsors has been tainted with controversy. It has always been true that Dover Hill country club, where the prestigious Champions invitational is played, accepts only men as members—but this year, the powerful Women's Rights Organization (WRO) has decided to make a bigger issue of that exclusivity.

Under pressure from the WRO to withdraw its support, Pace Sterling must think about the marketing value it gets from the sponsorship and how that value might be diminished—or heightened—by the controversy.

Executive Summary

Sandy firmly believes that Pace Sterling should stay the course and sponsor the event. The sponsorship makes good economic sense, she reasons, and the entire feel of it—its blend of prowess, privilege, and sheer class—is perfectly aligned with Pace Sterling's brand. What's more, many of the people who watch the tournament have the authority to make, or at least influence, a decision to go with the firm.

Sandy is unwavering until she sees this headline: "Tommy Ward Should Boycott Dover Hill." Ward is the king of the golf world and the favorite to win the Champions. The WRO is turning up the volume.

Should Pace Sterling proceed with its sponsorship? Offering advice on this fictional case are Sergio Zyman, former chief marketing officer of Coca-Cola; James E. Murphy, global managing director of marketing and communications at Accenture; Kim Skildum-Reid, coauthor of *The Sponsor's Toolkit* and *The Sponsorship Seeker's Toolkit*; and Paul A. Argenti, a professor of management and corporate communication at Dartmouth's Tuck School of Business.

"Nice drive," Duane Betts called out as the ball rolled to a halt a good three yards short of the 18th hole's infamous water hazard.

Sandy Michaels, chief marketing officer of the financial services giant Pace Sterling, stole a quick glance at the caddie. Even he seemed impressed. "Thanks, Duane," she smiled. "But watch me slice the next one into the clubhouse." Sandy was playing her best game in recent memory, but there was no point in boasting. She could never beat a veteran player like Duane, particularly on his home course.

"I don't know, I'd say you're having a great day all around," Duane drawled as he flashed her a quick wink. He was right. Sandy had already won the most important game—securing the exclusive sponsorship of the annual Professional Golf Organization's Champions Tournament for the 12th year in a row. Duane was in charge of corporate sponsorships, and he'd agreed to all of her terms. Her boss would be thrilled.

"Really, Duane, it's enough just to be out here on such a beautiful day." Sandy handed her driver to the caddie. "Ol' Mac McKinley sure knew what he was doing, didn't he?" She was referring to the man who designed the course nearly 70 years ago. His perfect combination of aesthetics and challenging play had made this course legendary—and ensured that it would become the perennial home of American golf's most prestigious invitational. "Honestly, I don't know how you get any work done. I'd want to be out here all day."

"It surely is a temptation," Duane agreed as they walked down the fairway. "And one to which some of my fellow club members do submit." Squinting to sight his ball, he added, "Though not of your gender, of course." Sandy flinched at the comment, a reminder that this grand old club, Dover Hill, didn't admit women as members. But she knew he meant no offense. An old-school southern gentleman, Duane was nothing if not gracious.

As he lined up his shot, he paused and glanced at her. "And it's even more beautiful in the spring. When those magnolias over there are in bloom," he said nodding at the row of trees lining the fairway, "it's simply delightful."

"Oh, I know, Duane," Sandy said with a smile. It would be beautiful in April when the tournament was held, all right. But better still would be the marketing mileage her company was going to get in the meantime.

A Good Walk Spoiled

A few weeks later, Sandy was in her office with her ad agency's creative team looking at initial concepts for the TV ads Pace Sterling would air. The company sponsored many events, sporting and otherwise, but the Champions was different. The whole feel of it—its blend of prowess, privilege, and sheer class—was perfectly aligned with Pace Sterling's brand. And just as perfect were the demographics of the tournament's viewers. Most of them had the authority to make, or at least influence, a decision to go with the firm.

A soft knock on the door interrupted her concentration. She looked up and grinned. It was Calvin Buckley, Pace Sterling's chairman and chief executive, just back from a week of international travel. "Hey, Cal, take a look," Sandy said excitedly as she gestured toward a lush-looking photograph of his favorite course. "Wouldn't you like to be *there* right now?"

She was surprised to see him grimace as he glanced down at it. "Actually, Sandy," he said, looking back up and meeting her eye, "this is exactly what I stopped by to talk about. I'm a little worried about this business with the WRO."

Sandy stared at him. The WRO, or Women's Rights Organization, was a powerful activist organization that had been pressuring Dover Hill to change its male-only membership. For years, the WRO had lobbied the club's many well-heeled, and for the most part well-intentioned, members to push internally for change. Recently, though, it had switched tactics and was trying to put the Professional Golfers Organization in the hot seat. Why, the WRO was publicly asking, was the PGO willing to let such a blatantly sexist organization host the most visible event of its tour?

Sandy asked the creative team to leave her office and closed the door. None of this was news, and besides, Cal had been happy with the sponsorship contract two weeks ago. Then she noticed the envelope he was holding out to her. Opening it, she fished out the cause of his concern: a letter from the WRO's chairwoman, Gillian Golding, taking him to task for his company's support of a discriminatory organization. Copies of the letter had also been sent to the national news media.

"This letter's pretty aggressive," Cal said as Sandy scanned it. "The WRO has always made their views on private clubs known, but they've usually had more important battles to fight." He cleared his throat. "I don't know," he said. "This year I think they're going to raise the volume on this one."

"Don't worry, Cal. I'll handle it," Sandy reassured him. "We'll bring them in for a meeting and explain that our relationship with the PGO is broader than the Champions. Dover Hill is just one of many venues they use, and the problem, if there is a problem, resides with the club, not the PGO—and certainly not us. Maybe I'll brief them on our diversity initiatives, too."

"I don't know, Sandy," Cal cautioned. "I don't think it's that simple. They're clearly focused on the Champions. We may want to rethink what we do."

"What are you saying, Cal? You're not suggesting we back out of the sponsorship, are you?" Sandy was surprised at how high her voice was.

"No," he said quickly. "Not necessarily. But," he added, glancing down at the boards on her table, "at the very least, we may want to ratchet down our visibility this year."

Sandy felt her face flush. "But the whole point is visibility, and I really don't see—"

"Sandy," Cal said raising his hands to interrupt her. "Listen to me." She took a deep breath. "I've been talking with our board, and I've promised them that we're going to be very thoughtful and deliberate about this. If the WRO makes a big deal out of our sponsorship, it could be an enormous PR liability for us. All I'm asking is that you make the case that we proceed."

"What do you want me to do?"

"Start with the assumption that the WRO is going to declare war on Dover Hill and the PGO, and that part of their strategy will be to try to force us into taking a public position. I want your read on how much that would diminish the value of our sponsorship."

"Or increase it," Sandy muttered, but she took his point. "Okay, Cal. I understand your concern. When do you want my analysis?"

"In a week?"

"Fine," she said. She wasn't too worried. It was only a letter—much ado about nothing. With all of the data her staff had compiled in advance of her negotiations with Duane, not to mention the results they'd garnered from previous Champions sponsorships, it should be a piece of cake.

Taking a Mulligan

By the time Sandy got home that evening, she'd already outlined her report for Cal. In addition to presenting all of the historical data about the value of the sponsorship, she would also include a discussion of the firm's target female audience. Yes, Pace Sterling had plenty of female customers and wanted even more, but it reached them through other means—including a variety of sports and cultural sponsorships. How many of them, outside the WRO's hard core of activists, were paying any attention to the Champions? And how many would shun Pace Sterling even if they were?

Sandy was standing in the kitchen arguing these points to her husband as he scanned the newspaper. "Besides," she said, vigorously chopping vegetables for a salad, "it isn't as if it's a scandal. Dover Hill hasn't done anything new or shocking. It's private, and it's been an all-male club since 1936. Steve, are you listening?"

"Since 1936," he repeated. "Of course I'm listening."

"Well, by that logic, the WRO should be attacking the Boy Scouts, too. Plus, we've been a sponsor since 1991, and no one has objected to our sponsorship before. So don't you think we might seem a little disingenuous—even hypocritical—if we were to suddenly turn around and side with the WRO? It's like that scene in *Casablanca*, where the guy says, 'I'm shocked, *shocked* to find that gambling is going on here!'"

"Louis Renault," interjected her husband, "played by Claude Rains."

"Right," she said. "The point is, it could even damage us if the public—or at least the golf-loving public—saw us reverse course and distance ourselves from the Champions. For golfers, Dover Hill is like Mecca."

"But darling," Steve mused, "times do change."

Sandy stopped chopping. "Yes? And so?"

Steve looked up from the newspaper. "And so attitudes change. You can do things the same way for years and look around one day and find you're out of step. Think of apartheid, for instance. It certainly wasn't a new policy in the 1980s, but the sentiment against it had reached a tipping point, so American companies just couldn't keep investing in South Africa. Eventually, it just became intolerable."

Sandy bristled at the analogy. "My company is not propping up some oppressive regime, Steve. Dover Hill isn't a public organization. It's a private club with the right to set its own rules. Let them set up a female-only golf club. The right of free assembly is in the

Constitution for God's sake!" She walked toward him with the salad bowl in her hand. The bang it made on the table signaled to Steve that the conversation was over.

Double Bogey

Three days later, Sandy ran into Cheryl Evans, Pace Sterling's head of human resources. "Sandy," Cheryl greeted her. "We were just talking about you and the Dover Hill controversy. Amazing, isn't it? I've just been preparing my report to Cal on it."

"*Your* report?" Sandy was taken aback. Why had Cal asked human resources to weigh in on what was clearly a marketing matter?

"Oh yes, he wanted my input, too," Cheryl said brightly. "It's a war out there trying to attract top women graduates and increase our percentage of female recruits every year. It's a war in here, too. We need to do much more to retain our women with high leadership potential. It'd really hurt us if we were perceived to have an old-boy kind of culture."

Sandy's expression was one of deep skepticism. "So you're saying that if we sponsor the Champions, women will feel they're not valued here?"

"Precisely," Cheryl said. "And I know Cal doesn't want that. Remember that speech he gave about renewing our commitment to diversity? Now I'm really on the hook to get some of those numbers up." She reached over and touched Sandy's arm, adding in mock desperation, "Please promise me you'll never leave."

Sandy couldn't help but smile. "Don't worry," she said. "I'm not going anywhere. But tell me, who else is Cal asking for input?"

"He's having lunch with some business ethics guru today to get his perspective. And of course he's asking the legal department to weigh in."

"Makes sense," Sandy conceded. "To find out what repercussions we might face if we back out of the sponsorship."

"Well, but also to say whether sticking with it could hurt us in any pending or future gender discrimination cases brought against us. You know lawyers," Cheryl continued on, rolling her eyes. "They'll use anything they can to demonstrate a pattern."

"It could just as easily blow over in a few months. What if the WRO comes up with some new cause célèbre and eases off?"

Sandy shook her head in annoyance. "Seems like people around here are really overreacting. I mean, even if the WRO does drag our name through the mud a little—which I'm not sure they'd do, given the other causes we support—does that mean we should give up a premium sponsorship? Which, by the way, one of our competitors would gladly snap up."

The last point caught Cheryl's interest. "They would?" she asked. "Don't you think Dover Hill is losing some serious cachet over this?"

"It might seem that way at the moment," Sandy said. "But it could just as easily blow over in a few months. What if the WRO comes up with some new cause célèbre and eases off? For that matter, who's to say Dover Hill won't have a change in leadership and decide to admit women next year? In the meantime, we'd have walked away from more than a decade-long relationship and left them in the lurch. Something tells me we wouldn't be welcomed back with open arms." She sighed, realizing that all these arguments would have to be addressed in her report. "I'm sorry, Cheryl, but I have to run. Thanks for your thoughts."

"But wait," Cheryl said. "Are you going to recommend to Cal that we move ahead with the sponsorship?"

"Absolutely."

"Well," Cheryl said as Sandy turned to leave, "good luck with that."

Let the Big Dog Eat

Cupping her hand over the phone, Sandy's assistant mouthed the name "Jack Spearwood," knowing from experience that Sandy might prefer she take a message.

Jack was Pace Sterling's head of new business development.

"Put him through," Sandy sighed, as she walked into her office and plopped down in her leather chair.

"Listen Sandy, I know it's still early," his voice boomed over the line. "But we need to figure out how we're going to allocate the Champions tickets. Last year, about 50 of them ended up going to waste. How can I make sure I get more of them into my people's hands this year so we can get some honest-to-God business out of it?" Sandy rolled her eyes. Every year there was a fight over the tickets, and Jack seemed to think every last one should go to the sales force to help them meet their quotas. Last year he was upset, for example, that Cal used eight tickets to host the governor and his family and that four tickets were donated to a charity benefit's silent auction.

Sandy dropped the bombshell. "Jack, I wish I could give you every ticket this year, I really do. But you know what? We might not get any." Even in her misery, she relished the moment of stunned silence that followed. Then she proceeded to fill him in on the situation.

Jack was predictably upset. "What?" he yelled. "Are you telling me we are caving in to a bunch of feminists who have nothing better to do than point fingers at who's not PC enough for their tastes? What's next, the vegetarian lobby? Are we going to stop serving meat in the cafeteria?"

Sandy winced. She never exactly enjoyed being on the same side as Jack—his views could be so extreme. But she hastened to assure him she was. "I'm giving Cal my report tomorrow," she said. "It's a strong recommendation to proceed with the sponsorship."

"Damn straight. Do you want me to go with you?"

"No, Jack," she said, picturing the scene. "That's okay. I can handle it."

Time to Lay Up?

Sandy rose early and went for a brisk two-mile run. Her report for Cal Buckley was complete, and she was happy with it. She had compiled all the relevant data about the reach and demographics of the Champions audience. She had assigned probabilities to the shifts in public perception that might occur if the WRO went on the offensive. She even addressed the HR concerns that Cheryl had raised. And, of course, she added Jack's support and comments, albeit toned down. Her bottom-line recommendations were clear, concise, and compelling—Pace Sterling should stay the course and sponsor this year's Champions event. It simply made good economic sense.

Back at the house, Sandy paused to pour a cup of coffee from the pot Steve had just brewed. Glancing down, she saw the morning paper, left open to the op-ed page. She nearly dropped her mug when she read the headline: "Tommy Ward Should Boycott Dover Hill." Ward, as Sandy and everyone else in America knew, was the undisputed king of the golf world—a phenomenon who had single-handedly made the sport cool to a whole new generation of potential players. He was also, not coincidentally, the odds-on favorite to win the Champions Tournament. But this influential paper was asking him to take a stand against discrimination.

Suddenly, Sandy felt far less confident about her recommendation to her boss. Given this new development, maybe she should beg off for another couple of days. On the other hand, it was nothing more than Cal had predicted: The WRO had turned up the volume. She gulped down her coffee and headed for the shower, now dreading the day before her. It would be a day where people at every turn would ask the same questions: How did she think Tommy Ward would respond? And what would that mean for Pace Sterling?

Should Pace Sterling Proceed with This Sponsorship?

Four commentators offer expert advice.

➤ Sergio Zyman

Sergio Zyman is the author of The End of Advertising as We Know It *(John Wiley & Sons, 2002). Before launching his consulting firm, Zyman Marketing Group, he was chief marketing officer of the Coca-Cola Company.*

The first question I ask when deciding whether to go forward with a sponsorship is, "Did it ever make sense in the first place?" So many don't. When I arrived at Coca-Cola, the joke there was, "If it stands still, paint it red, and if it moves, sponsor it." We were asked to sponsor everything from the Venice Flower Show to the *Titanic* exhibit. In the old days, we would have said, yes, yes, yes. But eventually, we learned to ask some hard questions like "Will it generate enough profits to at least equal the cost of sponsorship?"

We don't know how much Pace Sterling has paid to sponsor the Champions, but the partnership does seem good from an image-building standpoint. It has clearly offered substantial "associative equity"—that is, Pace Sterling has benefited from associating itself with the Champions by tapping into people's positive feelings about it. And the two brands appear to be compatible, which is critical in a high-profile sponsorship. At Coca-Cola, for example, we chose to have our Sprite brand sponsor the NBA because Sprite's slogan "Obey Your Thirst" was all about being your own person. The NBA had that same ethos at its core. It wouldn't have made sense for Sprite to sponsor, say, the NFL.

The Champions also serves Pace Sterling well in the firm's B2B selling efforts. If a decision maker at one of Pace Sterling's big institutional clients saw the company's logo on a backboard of some televised event, that might not be very relevant to that client. But if a Pace Sterling account manager offered that person premium tickets to an event he'd love to attend? Relevant.

There's another reason I think the Champions sponsorship has been a good one, and it has to do with the notion that there are four levels of sponsorship possible in sports marketing (and they probably have their equivalents in the arts, charity, and other targets of corporate support). At the lowest level, you can sponsor an individual player. At the next level, you can sponsor a team. One level higher would be to sponsor an event, or even a league. And the highest level is to sponsor a passion. To me, the Champions—golf's most prestigious invitational, we're told—is at that highest level. Even though it's a single event, it's an archetypal one because it captures so much of what golf lovers hold dear. The same is true of the Super Bowl for football fans.

It's always best to sponsor a passion. That's partly because people's associations are so pure and positive at that level. It's also because, as you descend through the four levels, your risks increase. Teams win and lose. If your team loses, the value of that association is diminished. Company sponsors feel that directly in sports like European soccer where their logos are displayed on the players' jerseys. Even more variable is the performance of individual players, on and off the field.

All of this means that, at a reasonable price, the Champions should have been a powerful marketing asset for Pace Sterling for many years to come. I can see why Sandy Michaels is reluctant to let go of this sponsorship.

But in the end, that's what she'll have to do. It's not worth attracting the ire of the WRO. If this were a live-or-die marketing investment for Pace Sterling, then yes, it would have to fight. But I can't imagine any sports sponsorship being that important to a company. And there are so many places to put sponsorship dollars—believe me, I know—that there's no need to tolerate a relationship that's causing your company pain.

It's unfortunate that Gillian Golding has decided to target this event to further a quite separate cause. But there it is. And I can tell you, in the real world, if the head of the nation's most powerful women's organization puts public pressure on you to walk away from a sponsorship, you walk.

➤ James E. Murphy

James E. Murphy is the global managing director of marketing and communications at Accenture in New York.

If I were in Sandy's position, I'd focus on some basic questions: What's the damage? Is it long lasting? Does the company believe this is an ethical issue? And can Pace Sterling wield some influence as a sponsor to improve the situation?

At Accenture, we've been longtime sponsors in three major areas: the arts, Formula One racing, and golf. In the arts, for example, we sponsored the 1998 Van Gogh exhibit in Washington, DC, and we're now the exclusive sponsor of the Manet/Velázquez exhibit at the Metropolitan Museum of Art. In Formula One, we sponsor the BMW WilliamsF1 Team and 17 race events. And in golf, we have our Accenture

Match Play Championship, which is part of a global series of four tournaments. We also sponsor several other televised golf events.

We value all these sponsorships for the same reasons: Our clients like the events, and the sponsorships are powerful brand builders. The events are excellent entertainment venues where our partners can spend relaxed and extended time with existing and prospective clients.

A good sponsorship arrangement provides other benefits, too. It can give added punch to your media buys. It can also help shape people's perceptions about your brand. For example, back in the early days of the Chicago Marathon—about 20 years ago—Beatrice Foods essentially bankrolled the entire event. Beatrice saw the association as particularly valuable because it was a means to promote the company's healthy food lines. Similarly, at Accenture, it's important to us to sponsor global sporting events because we want to underscore our firm's worldwide reach. In the Accenture Match Play Championship, we do just that. The event also allows us to show off some of our unique skills. Clients hire us for our ability to lead large-scale projects with complex logistics, many participants, and tightly managed timetables, and a well-run global golf tournament is an indicator of how we excel at such projects. It keeps the pressure on our global events team to do an impeccable job.

Primarily, though, an event like the Champions benefits Pace Sterling because it presents a client entertainment opportunity. When you're selling professional services in a business-to-business setting, personal relationships are vital. That's why, in the case study, we see the sales director campaigning so hard for those tickets. And that's also why it's absolutely essential for Sandy Michaels to get a sense of how the firm's clients feel about the controversy.

Why don't we see her fielding any surveys to do this? In another era, it might have been difficult to reliably gauge clients' attitudes in such a limited time frame, but not today. At Accenture, we make heavy use of the Internet to survey our market, and that would seem an obvious tactic in this case. At the very least, the report she's in the midst of preparing for her boss should emphasize the need for client input before Pace Sterling makes a decision.

Walking away from a long-standing sponsorship isn't an attractive option. Pace Sterling's involvement in the Champions has surely been cumulative in its effects. Abruptly cutting off that involvement would mean lower returns on all those years of marketing investment. So Sandy needs to ask a simple question: "Does management feel strongly about either side of the issue?" If it does, that should be the guiding position. If the feelings are ambiguous, then Sandy needs to ask a few more questions: "Is this an event that Pace Sterling's best clients want to be part of? Will the public accept the firm's role in the event? Will employees feel comfortable?" If the answers are no, she needs to cut her losses and find another venue.

➢ Kim Skildum-Reid

Kim Skildum-Reid is the coauthor of The Sponsorship Seeker's Toolkit *(McGraw-Hill, 1999) and* The Sponsor's Toolkit *(McGraw-Hill, 2001). Her consulting company, Skildum-Reid, provides advice and training to corporate sponsors around the world. She is based in Sydney, Australia.*

Now that consumers have come to understand their value to companies, they're expecting more from them. Years ago, these customers chose one brand over another on the basis of functional need and price. Now, because many product categories have become commodities in these two respects, buyers increasingly base their decisions on other factors such as emotional need and value alignment. How cool do you look wearing Nike sunglasses? How outdoorsy do you feel driving a Land Rover?

While a lot of marketing talks about these more emotional aspects, the right sponsorship actually demonstrates an emotional alignment with a target market. To a much greater extent than other marketing media, sponsorships communicate what the brand values, and how aligned that is with the values of its target markets. Herein lies the problem for Pace Sterling.

For Sandy Michaels, this sponsorship is only a targeted communications mechanism. She is buying into the outdated concepts of exposure and image transfer, and focusing on how well the event aligns with Pace Sterling's brand.

What she needs to worry about is how well it aligns with her market's target values. If a person loves animals, he will be more inclined to buy from a company that donates to the Humane Society, because his purchase from that company will say something about him. By the same token, a company that associates with a sexist organization is saying something about its own values—and its customers may not want to associate themselves with those beliefs.

Sandy and her sales chief Jack Spearwood are concerned about losing a tremendous hospitality opportunity for key clients. What they aren't taking into account is that the clients might not even show up. This issue is divisive, and the high-profile publicity and possible media and public outcry will make every client's decision to attend the event a political one within his own company. To a greater or lesser degree, the same thought process—What does this say about me?—will be repeated by customers, staff, potential recruits, and shareholders.

Sure, losing this event will leave a hole in Pace Sterling's portfolio, but that doesn't really concern me. Even if the sponsorship were getting big results, it may well have been getting stale after 12 years and providing diminishing returns. A lot of other events out there have similar cachet, reach the right market, and aren't going to make customers question Pace Sterling's or their own ethics.

Of course, getting out of the sponsorship could be tricky. The stated reason for making that break should be diminished value due to disrepute and disgrace. Consider the Olympic sponsorship during the scandals surrounding the

2000 and 2002 Games. Although there were no accusations of collusion or other direct damage to sponsors' reputations, the fact that the once sterling reputation of the Olympic movement had been tarnished made the $40 million price tag harder to justify. Since Pace Sterling was aware of the gender issue, it may be difficult for it to make a convincing argument. But even if there's no financial recourse, it should have zero marketing presence at the event.

The stickiest part will be deciding what to say to consumers, businesses, staff, media, and government. All of them will be asking, "Why didn't Pace Sterling drop its sponsorship long ago?" I suggest that the firm respond: "We have believed for some time, as the WRO did, that Dover Hill would see reason and join us in the twenty-first century. Unfortunately, that hasn't been the case."

Complacency is the cause of this mess. It's just too bad Pace Sterling didn't disassociate itself, or use its influence to quietly effect change, before the situation came to a head.

➤ Paul A. Argenti

Paul A. Argenti is Professor of Management and Corporate Communication and the director of the Tuck Leadership Forum at Dartmouth College's Tuck School of Business in Hanover, New Hampshire. He is the coauthor, with Janis Forman, of The Power of Corporate Communication *(McGraw-Hill, 2002).*

This story demonstrates what a favor Hootie Johnson did last fall for Citigroup, IBM, and Coca-Cola. These companies, of course, were the sponsors of the Masters Tournament being played this month at Augusta National—until Johnson, the chairman of that all-male club, announced that the event would not "request their participation" in 2003. The move saved those companies from the painful decision Pace Sterling must now make.

And it's clear to me what that decision should be. Pace Sterling shouldn't sponsor the tournament. Companies get involved in sponsorships primarily to enhance their reputations. They are leveraging someone else's credibility and image for their own benefit. Why take on the baggage of a partner whose reputation is compromised?

Precedent certainly exists for ending long-running sponsorship arrangements—and for similar reasons. Just a few years ago, IBM walked away from a 40-year relationship as a top Olympic sponsor in the wake of findings about corruption in its site-selection process. A company spokesperson said at the time, "The general cynicism the public has toward all institutions, they now have toward the Olympics." Pepsi-Cola decided back in 1968 to end its support of the Miss America contest after 11 years as a sponsor. Its stated reason? The event no longer represented the changing values of American society. Not coincidentally, this was not long after the formation of the National Organization for Women, and the first year that feminist protests of the event gained national media attention.

So what should Cal Buckley do? I would look at what Sandy Weill of Citigroup did regarding the Masters. Remember that Weill was really in the hot seat not only for being the chair of a sponsoring organization but also for being a member of Augusta National. His response was to break ranks with his club. He wrote a letter to Martha Burk, head of the National Council of Women's Organizations, stating his support for admitting women into Augusta National. He then went public with the letter. Ken Chenault of American Express did the same soon after.

It would be a mistake for Cal to stall. Sandy may be right that, soon enough, Dover Hill might well admit a female member and the whole thing could blow over. But she's wrong to think that her company's reputation would come out on the other side unscathed. Pace Sterling would always be the company that was on Dover Hill's side, when Dover Hill was on the wrong side.

Perhaps at the end of the case Sandy is beginning to see the light. If not, Cal should find a new CMO. Sandy lacks marketing savvy—particularly for the financial services industry, which is so risk-averse in matters of reputation. She needs to remember that her job isn't to teach a civics lesson on the right of free assembly but instead to enhance her company's reputation.

One thing this incident should teach her (and I'll admit it's a new lesson for most marketers) is the absolute need for due diligence in considering sponsorship opportunities. Sandy sees this controversy as a bolt from the blue, but in fact it could have been foreseen. Just as the WRO zeroed in on the problem, a marketer skilled in issues management could have anticipated it.

I'll reserve my last bit of advice for Dover Hill, which obviously must repair its own reputation. You need to do three things, guys—and fast. First, get rid of your chairman if he's been publicly defiant on the issue. No matter how decent a person he is, the public now sees him as the face of discrimination, and he's a liability. Second, apologize to those you've offended. At the very least, make a public statement along the lines of, "Traditions die hard, but we now realize times have changed." And third, for God's sake, get some female members in there!

Originally published in April 2003

Reprint R0304A

ABOUT THE CONTRIBUTORS

Bronwyn Fryer is a senior editor at HBR.

Dawn Iacobucci is the John J. Pomerantz Professor in Marketing at the Wharton School, University of Pennsylvania.

Brian A. Johnson is a senior research analyst at Sanford C. Bernstein & Co., an investment research and management firm in New York City.

Julia Kirby is editor, special issues, at HBR.

Paul F. Nunes is a senior research fellow at Accenture's Institute for Strategic Change, based in Cambridge, Massachusetts.

Anand P. Raman is a senior editor at HBR.

Thomas J. Waite serves as a strategic adviser to numerous organizations.